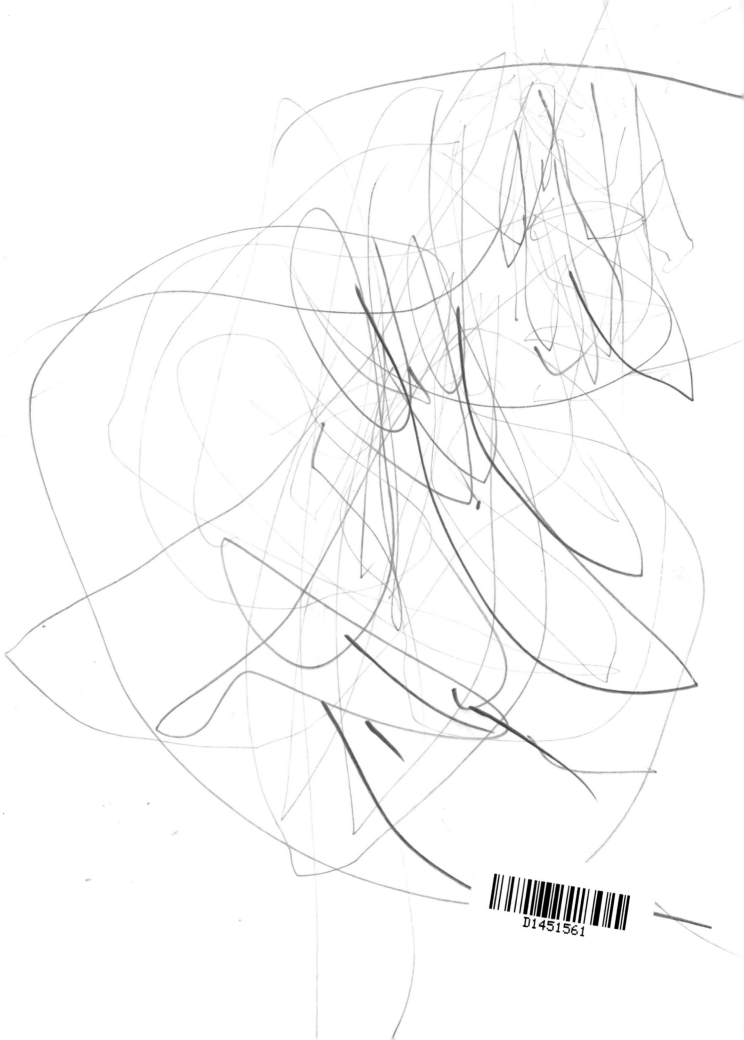

D1451561

LONGHORNS' PERFECT DRIVE

TEXAS' 2005 NATIONAL CHAMPIONSHIP SEASON

SPORTS PUBLISHING L.L.C.

SportsPublishingLLC.com

SPORTS PUBLISHING L.L.C.

SportsPublishingLLC.com

Austin American-Statesman

Peter L. Bannon publisher

Joseph J. Bannon Sr. publisher

Susan M. Moyer senior managing editor

Noah Adams Amstadter acquisitions editor

Doug Hoepker developmental editor

K. Jeffrey Higgerson art director

Dustin J. Hubbart cover design, imaging

Heidi Norsen interior layout, imaging

Erin Linden-Levy photo editor

Michael Laosa publisher

Belinda Gaudet executive vice president/general manager

Richard A. Oppel editor

Fred Zipp managing editor

John Bridges sports editor

G.W. Babb design director

Zach Ryall director of photography

ISBN (Hardcover): 1-59670-116-1   ISBN (Softcover): 1-59670-115-3   © 2006 Austin American-Statesman
Front cover photo by Ralph Barrera. Back cover photo by Deborah Cannon.
Printed in the United States of America
Sports Publishing L.L.C. 804 North Neil Street • Champaign, IL 61820 • Phone: 1-877-424-2665 • Fax: 217-363-2073

CONTENTS

Texas celebrates a 41-38 victory over USC at the 2006 Rose Bowl.
Jay Janner/American-Statesman

FOREWORD

KIRK BOHLS
AUSTIN AMERICAN-STATESMAN

Kirk Bohls has been sports columnist for the Austin American-Statesman *since 1994. A Central Texas native, he has been covering Longhorn football as a reporter, beat writer or columnist for 32 years.*

Time didn't stand still as Vince Young worked his magic one more time in the shadows of the majestic San Gabriel Mountains on a cool January evening and produced yet another of his signature, breath-taking moments in a career that has been full of them.

The long-anticipated outcome of the Rose Bowl only made the severe passage of time between national championships much more palatable.

Those closely involved with University of Texas football for the last half-century are all too aware of the near-misses and heartaches of the 35 seasons since the 1970 team claimed the school's third national championship.

Orangebloods everywhere keenly felt the disastrous conclusion of the 1977 season, where a perfect record dissolved in a Cotton Bowl meltdown against Notre Dame. Hearts broke again in the agonizing Cotton Bowl loss to huge underdog Georgia, tarnishing an otherwise spectacular, undefeated 1983 season for a star-studded Longhorn team that sent 21 players to NFL training camps the following summer.

In his first seven years at Texas, Mack Brown's teams stacked one outstanding season upon another, only to fall short of the ultimate prize. This Rose Bowl was more than a historic matchup of two marquee college football programs that had been literally joined at the hip at the top of the national polls since August.

This Rose Bowl was a shot at sweet redemption, at proper validation of a team that couldn't win the big game, a coach who had never won a conference title in his first 21 seasons at three different schools, a storied program that hadn't lately measured up against schools with similar pedigrees.

All that changed, all those disappointments were flushed away, in one glorious evening in California as the Longhorns dethroned the two-time defending national champion—a team that had won 34 consecutive games—to capture a fourth national crown for the University of Texas.

Time did not stop. And neither did Young, the most gifted quarterback in the 112-year history of the school. Texas' victory capped a perfect season built on the foundation of another Rose Bowl victory on this very same field 12 months earlier against a powerful Michigan team. In that game, the Longhorns steeled themselves against the Wolverine onslaught and hammered out both a comeback for the ages and the starting point for a perfect 2005 season.

From the Rose Bowl victory over Michigan came confidence and a rigorous work ethic fashioned around intense workouts in the off-season. "Every Tuesday and Thursday of the summer, we'd be out there throwing the football around," junior safety Michael Griffin recalled. "If you didn't show up, you'd get a phone call. One time, Vince called me and said, 'Where were you?' It showed that everybody cared."

When the season began, the Longhorns were ready. They proved their merit in early September, rallying late in the game to defeat fourth-ranked Ohio State. A month later, they ended a devastating, five-year losing streak to Oklahoma.

In the weeks that would follow, the Longhorns showed just how talented and determined they were. When Oklahoma State jumped out to a big lead, the Longhorns rallied for a dramatic, come-from-behind win. When Texas A&M tried to carve out an upset at Thanksgiving, the Longhorns simply refused to be derailed.

Finally, in its rematch against Colorado, Texas made a huge statement, trouncing the Buffaloes, winning the Big 12 Championship and clinching a second consecutive trip to the Rose Bowl.

In Pasadena, the Longhorns made history—not by remaking themselves but by repeating what they had been doing every Saturday from September to December.

With four first-team All-Americans, Heisman runner-up Vince Young and a gritty defense, Texas stood powerful and proud in the face of a program that had been pronounced a modern-day dynasty. To win, they overcame a team with the last two Heisman Trophy winners, an exalted head coach and an offense considered by some to be one of the most prolific in the history of college football.

When all was said and done, the Texas Longhorns had secured the 800th victory in school history, an achievement that ranks third all-time behind only Michigan and Notre Dame.

They were perfect at 13-0. And they were Number 1.

It was time.

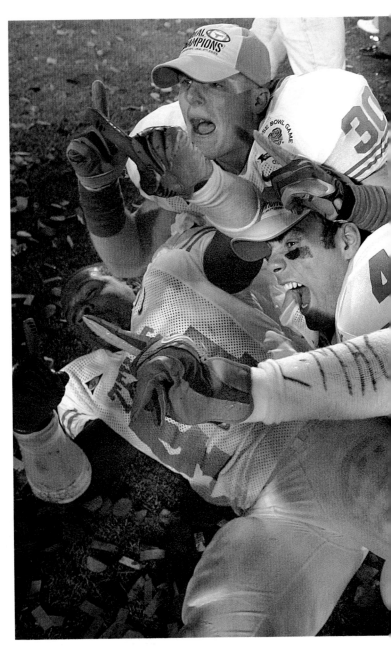

ABOVE: Rashad Bobino (44), Braden Johnson (30) and Eric Hall (49) celebrate on the field after the Longhorns beat USC in the Rose Bowl.

Deborah Cannon/American-Statesman

A RUGGED ROAD TO THE ROSE BOWL

BY KEVIN ROBBINS
AUSTIN AMERICAN-STATESMAN

The run for the roses starts right now. The No. 2-ranked Texas Longhorns attend to Louisiana-Lafayette tonight at Royal-Memorial Stadium. But what happens in a week might determine where they play in January.

A happy ending at No. 6 Ohio State could launch the Longhorns into Big 12 play with the momentum to beat Oklahoma for the first time since 1999, turn away a resurgent Texas A&M and land in Pasadena, Calif., to defend their title at the Rose Bowl. This time, the oldest bowl game in America determines a national champion.

"This is a great time of year for football programs across the country," Texas head coach Mack Brown said.

It's also a great time for Austin. The five home games of 2005 will bring an estimated $90 million to the local economy, according to the Austin Convention & Visitors Bureau.

ABOVE: **Texas players gather during one of the team's first practices.** Jay Janner/American-Statesman

"At our school, (the players) are scrutinized and they put up with a lot of things before they have proven themselves. That will be one of the question marks going into the first game: how well will they play under the microscope?"

–Texas head coach Mack Brown

OPPOSITE PAGE: Vince Young goes through drills during a practice.
Jay Janner/American-Statesman

Nearly four of 10 fans at home games are from out of town, and 80 percent of them stay in Austin's 25,000 hotel rooms, the bureau estimates.

It's been nine months since Texas kicker Dusty Mangum willed a last-second, last-prayer field goal over the crossbar at the Rose Bowl to vanquish Michigan.

Talk of a return to Pasadena has been going on that long, too. Texas lost its two marquee seniors, tailback Cedric Benson and linebacker Derrick Johnson, to the NFL. But slippery quarterback Vince Young—whose feats that night baffled Michigan defenders and awed college football followers all the way to the Downtown Athletic Club—returns behind a sturdy offensive line.

Selvin Young, a junior who broke his ankle last season, assumes Benson's old position in the backfield.

"I have been waiting for this moment since I walked on the University of Texas campus," he said. "It is a long time coming."

Added Vince Young, Selvin's roommate: "Everybody knows what he can do."

The Longhorns take the field tonight in a vintage uniform that conjures the national champions Darrell Royal coached. Black shoes on their feet, numbers on their helmets—so what if it's only for the first game? The throwback look sets a tone for the season. The reference is unmistakable: This is the year Texas returns to the top.

"Those are the guys who started this tradition and honor," said senior guard Will Allen.

After Ohio State, the Longhorns come home for Rice, and two weeks later go to Missouri. They play the Sooners on Oct. 8 for the 100th time in Dallas.

Then comes the rest of the conference schedule: Colorado, Texas Tech, Oklahoma State, Baylor and Kansas. Texas could arrive at Kyle Field to play the Aggies with a Big 12 title in the balance.

An undefeated season?

In Texas, there's always talk of an undefeated season.

But that hasn't happened since 1969, when the Red River Shootout was a much younger

ABOVE: During their final public scrimmage as part of Fan Appreciation Day, Ramonce Taylor (11) scampers past Brandon Foster.
Ralph Barrera/American-Statesman

OPPOSITE PAGE: Coach Mack Brown talks things over with cornerback Brandon Foster.
Jay Janner/American-Statesman

phenomenon and the Game of the Century ended when the Arkansas Razorbacks lost in front of a hometown crowd. Texas won in a 15-14 classic that has reached nearly mythological proportions. A month later, after dispatching Notre Dame in the Cotton Bowl, the Longhorns were 11-0.

The 2005 season is full of hazards. Ohio State. Oklahoma. Texas A&M. Texas Tech, Kansas and Oklahoma State would love to spoil.

Assurances? There are none.

"You can work on everything in scrimmages, but until you are tackled by someone you have never met who is in a different-colored uniform, it is hard to know how everyone will react," Brown said. "At our school, (the players) are scrutinized and they put up with a lot of things before they have proven themselves. That will be one of the question marks going into the first game: how well will they play under the microscope?"

Everything magnifies now. "We told them at the end of practice that you work 352 days for 13 Saturdays," Brown said. "This is their first chance to be seen as this football team. It's an exciting time."

And a defining one.

GAME 1: **TEXAS 60** LOUISIANA-LAFAYETTE 3

September 3, 2005
Darrell K Royal-Texas Memorial Stadium
Austin, Texas

YOUNG AND FRESH

BY SUZANNE HALLIBURTON
AUSTIN AMERICAN-STATESMAN

First games often can be ugly affairs, with incessant penalties, young players confused about where to line up, and special teams stumbling their way downfield. It's enough to leave the coach of a national championship contender with a permanent grimace on his face.

That wasn't the case Saturday night at Royal-Memorial Stadium as second-ranked Texas kicked off a promising season with a 60-3 victory over Louisiana-Lafayette.

The game was so lopsided that Texas coach Mack Brown benched his starters after the first series of the third quarter, then sent in the reserves to run mostly vanilla running plays for the rest of the game in hopes of keeping down the score.

There were no grimaces as Brown trotted to the locker room, only confident smiles.

"These games can scare you to death," Brown said. "And sometimes you end up like this and you say to yourself, 'What was I worried about?'"

"I felt like this was the perfect opener for us."

RIGHT: **Wearing a 1963-era throwback jersey in the opening game against Louisiana-Lafayette, Texas' Jamaal Charles carries the ball during the third quarter.**
Deborah Cannon/American-Statesman

With a matchup with No. 6 Ohio State six days away, the positives in Texas' nine-touchdown performance were almost too numerous to count.

About the only weaknesses were in the kicking game. In the first half, Richmond McGee missed three extra points, including two that were blocked, but seemed to have his problems fixed by intermission.

But every other aspect of the performance met Brown's expectations. The offense amassed 591 yards—400 by halftime—with the greatest production coming from the youngest legs of the team.

Freshman Jamaal Charles ran for 135 yards and one touchdown, the best debut for a first-year running back in program history. He broke the record set last year by Ramonce Taylor, who has turned into a combination tailback-receiver this season and accounted for 88 yards and one touchdown Saturday.

Meantime, 270-pound Henry Melton, who has been slotted for short-yardage work, steamrolled through a tiring Lafayette line for 65 yards on six carries and two touchdowns.

On his final score, which concluded the Longhorns' nine-touchdown run with 14:13 to play, Melton broke at least five tackles as he plowed the 22 yards to the end zone.

Junior Selvin Young, who started at tailback, managed 67 yards on eight carries with a touchdown. He did most of his work early in the game, then spent the remainder of the contest on the bench near midfield. He did send a scare through the crowd of 82,519 when, favoring his left ankle, he gingerly stepped to the sideline in the first quarter.

Young missed 11 games last fall after snapping his right fibula against Arkansas on a kickoff return. However, late Saturday, he wasn't even wearing a brace on his tender ankle.

All told, the Longhorn runners averaged a whopping 8 yards a carry. And at least on Saturday night, the Texas runners looked up to the task of taking some of the pressure off of Longhorns do-it-all quarterback Vince Young. He didn't rush as many

	1st	2nd	3rd	4th	Final
Louisiana-Lafayette	3	0	0	0	3
Texas	13	26	14	7	60

Scoring Summary

1st– **Texas** S. Young 9-yard run (McGee kick failed)–6 plays, 35 yards in 1:44.
La.-Laf. Comiskey 47-yard field goal–7 plays, 39 yard in 3:04.
Texas Charles 14-yard run (McGee kick)–7 plays, 65 yards in 2:24.

2nd– **Texas** Jones 10-yard pass from V. Young (McGee kick blocked)–8 plays, 56 yards in 3:17.
Texas Taylor 30-yard run (McGee kick blocked)–4 plays, 91 yards in 2:24.
Texas Thomas 20-yard pass from V. Young (McGee kick)–1 play, 20 yards in 0:06.
Texas Thomas 7-yard pass from V. Young (McGee kick)–7 plays, 60 yards in 2:40.

3rd– **Texas** V. Young 2-yard run (McGee kick)–4 plays, 10 yards in 1:19.
Texas Melton 14-yard run (Pino kick)–6 plays, 34 yards in 2:11.

4th– **Texas** Melton 22-yard run (Pino kick)–5 plays, 77 yards in 1:25.

Team Statistics

Category	La.-Laf.	Texas
First Downs	11	30
Rushes-Yards (Net)	34-72	52-418
Passing-Yards (Net)	166	173
Passes Att-Comp-Int	33-16-1	17-13-1
Total Offense Plays-Yards	67-238	69-591
Punt Returns-Yards	0-0	5-106
Kickoff Returns-Yards	5-91	1-34
Interception Returns-Yards	1-11	1-4
Punts (Number-Avg)	10-40.1	2-46.0
Fumbles-Lost	2-0	4-1
Sacks By (Number-Yards)	0-0	3-22
Penalties-Yard	10-83	7-55
Possession Time	31:19	28:41

times as the backs, but Young still gained 49 yards on seven carries.

He was most effective with his arm, completing 13 of 17 passes for 173 yards and three touchdowns—two to tight end David Thomas and the first to Nate Jones.

Of his four incompletions, one was dropped and another was intercepted near the Lafayette end zone. But Brown said the interception likely was more the fault of the intended receiver than it was a poor throw by the quarterback.

OPPOSITE PAGE: Texas tight end David Thomas (16) smiles after scoring a touchdown in the second quarter against Louisiana-Lafayette. Texas offensive guard Will Allen (72) congratulates him.
Brian K. Diggs/American-Statesman

"We wanted to send a message to the entire team about what we're trying to accomplish this year," the quarterback said.

The recrafted defense also made a four-star debut. With new coordinator Gene Chizik calling plays from the press box, Texas stayed in its base 4-3 defense the entire game and easily kept Jerry Babb, the Ragin' Cajuns' athletic quarterback, in check. The intent was so purposely keep the exotic blitzes in the playbook to as not to tip off Ohio State of any changes from a year ago.

The Longhorns allowed 238 yards, with only 99 of those coming against the starters. Defensive tackle Rod Wright started the Longhorns' onslaught with an 8-yard sack of Babb. And by game's end, freshman defensive end Chris Brown had a similar play, when he sacked reserve quarterback Michael Desormeaux for a 7-yard loss.

"We did a lot of good things," said middle linebacker Aaron Harris. "We believe there are things we can do better. But overall, I think we had a pretty good game."

OPPOSITE PAGE: Freshman Jamaal Charles outruns the Louisiana-Lafayette defense during the third quarter. Charles tallied 135 yards on 14 carries in his UT debut. *Deborah Cannon/American-Statesman*

BELOW: The Texas defense, led by Aaron Harris (2), Rodrique Wright (90), Brian Robison (39) and Tim Crowder (80), sacks Ragin' Cajun quarterback Jerry Babb during the first quarter.
Ralph Barrera/American-Statesman

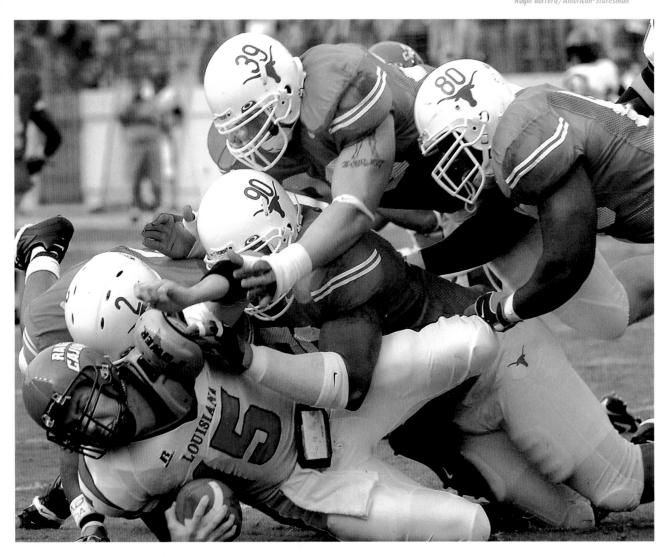

HOW SWEED

BY SUZANNE HALLIBURTON
AUSTIN AMERICAN-STATESMAN

Texas quarterback Vince Young could be magnanimous in victory Saturday night. After all, his late touchdown toss to Limas Sweed gave his team a 25-22 win over fourth-ranked Ohio State in a game that made his Longhorns a significant challenger to defending national champion Southern California.

So Young had no problems seeking out Buckeyes free safety Nate Salley, who was beaten on the throw in the left corner of the end zone to put Texas up 23-22 with 2 minutes, 37 seconds to play. Young gave him a friendly bear hug.

Next on Young's list to embrace was Ohio State quarterback Troy Smith, who was sacked by Rod Wright and Aaron Harris in the end zone for a game-clinching safety with 19 seconds to play. And at midfield just before Young turned to celebrate the "Eyes of Texas," he searched for Ted Ginn, the now-former Heisman Trophy candidate who was no factor in the game.

The ever-relaxed Young laughed in the interview room. Such dramatics have been his style.

"Basically, we've been through this before," Young said.

RIGHT: Limas Sweed makes the game-winning catch, a 24-yard pass from Vince Young, over Ohio State's Nate Salley in Columbus, Ohio.
Deborah Cannon/American-Statesman

ABOVE: Tim Crowder sacks Ohio State quarterback Troy Smith in the first quarter. *Matt Rourke/American-Statesman*

OPPOSITE PAGE: Texas' Vince Young and teammates celebrate a 25-22 victory over Ohio State. *Matt Rourke/American-Statesman*

Just when most in the stadium-record crowd of 105,565 fans thought that the Buckeyes had beaten No. 2 Texas and had finally controlled the dynamic quarterback like no other team, Young silenced them with a seven-play, 67-yard touchdown drive.

Although the Ohio State linebackers probably were the most formidable Young has ever played against, he stood back in the pocket, faked a handoff to running back Jamaal Charles, looked for tight end David Thomas, then found Sweed half a body length ahead of Salley for the score. It was the first time the Buckeyes had used that type of zone coverage in the game.

The victory was Texas' first over a top 10 team since defeating fourth-ranked Nebraska, 24-20 at Royal-Memorial Stadium in 1999. Since that last victory, the Longhorns have gone 0-8 against top 10 opposition. It was Ohio State's first home non-conference loss since 1990.

In beating Ohio State Saturday night, Texas needed to overcome three turnovers, including two interceptions by Young, and poor play from the Longhorns' kickoff coverage teams.

Ohio State had stunning field position, with eight possessions starting from outside its own 40. But the Buckeyes, after going down 10-0 in the first

quarter, could manage only five field goals and a touchdown, despite starting five drives within the Longhorns' 35.

As Brown started talking about his team's victory in the postgame interview session, he choked up and had to pause to keep his emotions in check.

"At times, we didn't even play very good, but we played hard and we believed," Brown said. "And we played with confidence and that's what we told the guys in the dressing room. Very seldom can you give up three turnovers like that and still win the game. But our guys kept coming back, and kept coming back and believing in each other and gave themselves a chance to win in the end."

It was Young's arm rather than his legs that proved to be the difference. He completed 18 of 29 passes for 270 yards, 130 of which went to Billy Pittman.

He also was Texas' leading rusher, netting 76 yards.

With Ohio State up 22-16 with about six minutes to go in the fourth quarter, the defense kept Texas in the game with three significant plays. They already had held Ginn to only seven yards of offense and limited an explosive Ohio State offense to five field goals and a touchdown.

First, end Brian Robison deflected a pass into the hands of Ohio State tailback Antonio Pittman, who lost four yards to the Texas 33. That took Josh Huston, who had a career-best five field goals, out of his comfort range. His 50-yard field goal attempt with five minutes to play sailed just to the right.

After Young connected with Sweed, the defense finally forced Ohio State's lone turnover of the evening. Justin Zwick pitched to Pittman, who was met by linebacker Drew Kelson. The sophomore, who missed out on two earlier interceptions, swatted the ball away, with the fumble recovered by Robison at the Ohio State 21.

Texas ran down the clock, going for fourth down from the 1. Although freshman Henry Melton was kept from the end zone, it left the Buckeyes with 99 yards to go with only 19 seconds remaining. Texas used a four-man rush against Smith on first down, followed by a freelancing Harris. Wright and Harris met Smith in the end zone to start the celebration.

"It was so exciting," Kelson said. "We didn't want to go back to the dressing room. We wanted to stay on the field and enjoy it."

	1st	2nd	3rd	4th	Final
Texas	10	3	3	9	25
Ohio State	0	16	6	0	22

Scoring Summary

1st– **Texas** Pino 42-yard field goal–11 plays, 64 yards in 3:54.

Texas Pittman 5-yard pass from V. Young (Pino kick)–10 plays, 84 yards in 4:03.

2nd–**Ohio St.** Huston 45-yard field goal–5 plays, 8 yards in 2:13.

Ohio St. Holmes 36-yard pass from Smith (Huston kick)–9 plays, 80 yards in 3:25.

Ohio St. Huston 36-yard field goal–4 plays, 1 yard in 1:55.

Ohio St. Huston 25-yard field goal–9 plays, 22 yards in 3:14.

Texas Pino 37-yard field goal–4 plays, 34 yards in 0:29.

3rd–**Ohio St.** Huston 44-yard field goal–6 plays, 11 yards in 2:33.

Texas Pino 25-yard field goal–7 plays, 72 yards in 4:10.

Ohio St. Huston 26-yard field goal–7 plays, 45 yards in 2:16.

4th–**Texas** Sweed 24-yard pass from V. Young (Pino kick)–7 plays, 67 yards in 2:23.

Texas Team safety.

Team Statistics

Category	Texas	Ohio St.
First Downs	19	13
Rushes-Yards (Net)	38-112	36-111
Passing Yards (Net)	270	144
Passes Att-Comp-Int	29-18-2	26-14-0
Total Offense Plays-Yards	67-382	62-255
Punt Returns-Yards	1-1	1-8
Kickoff Returns-Yards	4-91	6-191
Interception Returns-Yards	0-0	2-24
Punts (Number-Avg)	4-38.0	4-39.5
Fumbles-Lost	4-1	3-1
Sacks By (Number-Yards)	4-20	3-15
Penalties-Yards	4-30	8-78
Possession Time	30:09	29:51

ABOVE: Billy Pittman scores in the first quarter on a five-yard pass from Vince Young. Pittman was Texas' leading receiver with 130 yards on five catches.

Deborah Cannon/American-Statesman

HIS OWN WORST CRITIC

BY CEDRIC GOLDEN, *AUSTIN AMERICAN-STATESMAN*

SEPTEMBER 16, 2005

The phone rang as expected at the Sweed household in Washington around midnight Saturday.

Limas Sweed Sr. and wife Evelyn had not made the trip to Columbus, Ohio, but a dozen or so family members came to their house that night, eyes glued to the screen as the Texas Longhorns were driving in the fourth quarter.

When Vince Young's touchdown pass found the hands of a leaping receiver in the end zone, the place erupted. The screams reached another decibel level when they noticed that the receiver was wearing No. 4.

It was Limas.

There stood Limas Sweed, Jr., getting knocked around by his buddies in celebration after catching a touchdown for the first time in 13 career games. The score and extra point gave Texas a lead it would not relinquish.

The catch had made Sweed an instant hero—the play that Longhorns fans will recall forever from the historic first meeting of national powers Texas and Ohio State.

The phone call should have been one of triumph, of relief. One of a 20-year-old kid describing the biggest play of his life to parents who on the following day would receive newspapers from all over the country featuring their son in photographs and headlines.

It wasn't.

"Limas was really frustrated because he didn't think he had done enough," Evelyn Sweed recalled. "I said, 'Limas, don't you know what you just did? Baby, that catch won the game."

Cornerbacks and safeties represent Sweed's biggest obstacles in between the lines. Off the field, he is in a constant battle with an opponent far more challenging than a defensive back.

Himself.

"I hold myself to a certain standard," the soft-spoken Sweed said this week. "Anytime a guy wants to reach a certain goal, he has to be his own worst critic, especially when he is striving for perfection."

Sweed thought the University of Texas would be like high school in Brenham, but he was in for a wake-up call.

First there was Roy Williams. The comparisons began as soon as Sweed arrived in Austin. The similarities in height, build and gait were unmistakable. Williams had rewritten the UT record book for receivers and now it seemed he was being recreated through Sweed.

"I can't tell you how people told me how much I looked like Roy," Sweed said.

ABOVE: Off the field, Limas Sweed faces his toughest competition: himself.
Rodolfo Gonzalez/American-Statesman

BEYOND Xs AND Os

ABOVE: Texas' Limas Sweed catches a pass during the second quarter against Colorado's Tyrone Henderson to set up a touchdown. *Deborah Cannon/American-Statesman*

Their resumes were nearly identical: high school stars in multiple sports with great speed who ended up at Texas. As if the pressure of his own expectations was not enough, Sweed went to Williams before his redshirt freshman season and asked if he could wear Williams' No. 4. Williams agreed.

"He already had a lot of pressure on him because everybody was saying he was the next Roy," said roommate Brian Carter, the Longhorns' other starting receiver. "I told him not to worry what others think of him and just do the best you can."

Others thought the world of him in high school.

Sweed was to football what Dustin Majewski was to baseball at Brenham High. Sweed caught 72 passes in his last three seasons, and 31 of those went for touchdowns. The high school All-American had can't-miss numbers entering college and he had three good teachers in teammates Williams, B.J. Johnson, and Sloan Thomas.

The trio left after the 2003 season, and while Sweed did not have a spectacular freshman season as Williams had, he did finish with a respectable 23 catches for 263 yards. During the times he struggled, the support system was in place.

"He dropped a pass in one game, and you could see it was killing him," said close friend and teammate Tim Crowder. "I went over to him and let him know it wasn't the end of the world. You have to watch Limas because he gets real down on himself. It's all about confidence with him."

Accustomed to going back home before the summer, Sweed, the son of a Catholic church deacon, has spent the past two off-seasons working with Young and the other receivers in 7-on-7 drills conducted by the players. His work has drawn praise from receivers coach Bobby Kennedy, who

> ## "He already had a lot of pressure on him because everybody was saying he was the next Roy. I told him not to worry what others think of him and just do the best you can."
>
> –Brian Carter, Longhorn receiver

refers to Sweed, Nate Jones and Tyrell Gatewood as big bodies with good hands who can stretch the field.

Sweed could not have picked a better time to introduce himself to the end zone. Saturday's game-tying touchdown could be a springboard to big performances in future games, something that would suit the Longhorns just fine. Sweed hopes the play will bring a little noise to what he describes as a "quiet career."

"It will rack up his confidence a whole lot," Young said. "It will let him know he can make those types of plays all the time. With his size and physical ability, he can do it."

The day after the Ohio State game, Sweed called his parents after he noticed that he had 40 missed calls and 35 text messages on his cell phone from friends, family and strangers alike congratulating him on the catch.

"I guess I did do something," he said.

CHARLES IN CHARGE

BY SUZANNE HALLIBURTON
AUSTIN AMERICAN-STATESMAN

It seems that Jamaal Charles, the dazzling Texas tailback, still needs approval from his elders. After each series Saturday night in a 51-10 thrashing of Rice, the 18-year-old would trot over to quarterback Vince Young on the sideline and ask the same question.

"How'd I do?" Charles would inquire.

Young always told him the same thing. "Just fine."

In the huddle late in the first quarter, Young wanted to make sure his starting tailback had the energy to carry the ball for the fourth consecutive time on the series. And then he added some advice.

"He told me to keep running fast," Charles said of his conversation with the quarterback, "to pick up my legs and keep running fast."

Young handed him the ball, and Charles sprinted to the end zone, stiff-arming defenders for the final steps of his 25-yard run for the second of his three touchdowns.

A first-time starter, Charles played one series into the third quarter, gaining 189 yards on 16 carries. By then, the Longhorns had built a 45-0 lead. Only Cedric Benson, who gained 213 yards against Kansas in 2001, posted a better game for a Texas freshman. Charles' three TDs tied Butch Hadnot's freshman record.

The way Charles is playing—this is his second 100-yard rushing performance in three games—folks around Austin aren't missing Benson, a first-round NFL draft pick, as much as first thought.

Charles and an opportunistic defense provided the buzz on a sultry Saturday night, a week after the Longhorns knocked off then-fourth-ranked Ohio State 25-22. Texas was a nearly 41-point favorite over Rice, and with the outcome never in doubt, Charles proved to be the big story.

The charismatic Young, who keyed the Longhorns' electrifying victory over the Buckeyes, had a pedestrian evening. The Heisman candidate

OPPOSITE PAGE: **Jamaal Charles eludes the Rice defense and heads toward the end zone. Charles scored three touchdowns in 16 carries and ran for 189 total yards.**
Kelly West/American-Statesman

ABOVE: Ramonce Taylor (11) and Jamaal Charles (25) sing "The Eyes of Texas" following their 51-10 win over Rice. *Deborah Cannon/American-Statesman*

OPPOSITE PAGE: Vince Young rushed for 77 yards against the Owls. *Kelly West/American-Statesman*

completed 8 of 14 passes for 101 yards and ran for 77 yards on eight carries. Like Charles, he took to the sidelines and hung out with the first-team wideouts beginning with 10 minutes to go in the third quarter.

Young said he had no problems pushing the spotlight Charles' way. Charles made his first start because Selvin Young, the quarterback's roommate and best friend, still was suffering the lingering effects of a sprained left ankle.

"Just to see him carrying the ball, I was so proud," Vince Young said of Charles. "For him to run up and down the field like that, for him to be making plays, I was so proud. Today, it was his turn. In the future, it'll be my turn."

No. 2 Texas, with a bye next Saturday, improved to 3-0. The Longhorns start Big 12 Conference play Oct. 1, against Missouri. Rice, which didn't score until late in the third quarter, dropped to 0-2 after opening against UCLA a week ago.

Texas showed its dominance over the outmanned Owls midway through the first quarter. After Rice pulled off a special-teams coup, killing a

ABOVE: Frank Okam (97) dives for a loose ball in the Rice end zone. Okam recovered the fumble for a second-quarter touchdown.

Kelly West/American-Statesman

punt at the Longhorn 1-inch line, it took Texas all of seven plays to travel the 99 yards to put its lead at 14-0. Young had his longest gain of the season with a 51-yard scamper on a third-and-7 play from the Longhorns' 4. Then Charles gained 12, 3, 5 and 25 yards on the next four carries.

"Jamaal played exactly like we thought he would," said Texas offensive coordinator Greg Davis. "He is a special freshman. Football comes easy for him."

However, Charles didn't even know he was starting until someone told him to head out to the field after the opening kickoff. Selvin Young, who sprained an ankle late in preseason workouts, dressed for the game, but came out of the locker room in a cap rather than a helmet.

Charles was the obvious star for the offense. The defense also helped out the cause.

Michael Huff scored his fifth career touchdown with 10:07 to go in the second quarter to increase the Longhorns' lead to 21-0. Joel Armstrong pitched wide to Quinton Smith, and Huff, who was playing the halfback, picked up the ball on the first bounce and ran the final 21 yards for the score.

Then later in the second quarter, middle linebacker Aaron Harris sacked backup quarterback Chase Clement in the end zone. The fumble was recovered by defensive tackle Frank Okam.

Henry Melton and Ramonce Taylor each scored touchdowns after the Longhorns' defense blew open the game. David Pino also had a 40-yard field goal.

Texas coach Mack Brown was worried that his team would have a Buckeye hangover, given all the national hype that was heaped on the nationally televised prime-time game last Saturday night. He said his team only had "average" practices throughout this week in preparing for the Owls.

"We were still talking about Ohio State too much, and I was really concerned," Brown said. "But I thought we played really, really hard. I thought we played really, really well."

His players scattered into the night, knowing they wouldn't have to work out again until Tuesday.

Charles was asked if he was the celebratory kind.

He shook his head. His idea of a party is playing video games or reading a book in his dorm room. He said he'd probably go to church this morning.

"My people raised me well," Charles said.

And no one from Texas was doubting that.

	1st	2nd	3rd	4th	Final
Rice	0	0	3	7	10
Texas	14	28	9	0	51

Scoring Summary

1st— **Texas** Charles 25-yard run (Pino kick)—6 plays, 80 yards in 1:49.

Texas Charles 25-yard run (Pino kick)—7 plays, 99 yards in 3:12.

2nd— **Texas** Charles 4-yard run (Pino kick)—6 plays, 68 yards in 2:38.

Texas Huff 21-yard fumble recovery (Pino kick).

Texas Okam 0-yard fumble recovery (Pino kick).

Texas Melton 1-yard run (Pino kick)—7 plays, 70 yards in 1:50.

3rd— **Texas** Pino 40-yard field goal—7 plays, 40 yards in 2:10.

Rice Landry 37-yard field goal—8 plays, 39 yards in 4:13.

Texas Taylor 10-yard run (Pino kick failed)—4 plays, 33 yards in 1:46.

4th— **Rice** Clement 2-yard run (Landry kick)—9 plays, 71 yards in 3:53.

Team Statistics

Category	Rice	Texas
First Downs	12	24
Rushes-Yards (Net)	46-110	47-361
Passing Yards (Net)	99	122
Passes Att-Comp-Int	15-4-0	18-11-1
Total Offense Plays-Yards	61-209	65-483
Punt Returns-Yards	0-0	4-15
Kickoff Returns-Yards	6-104	1-31
Interception Returns-Yards	1-0	0-0
Punts (Number-Avg)	7-44.3	4-47.0
Fumbles-Lost	3-2	2-0
Sacks By (Number-Yards)	1-7	2-17
Penalties-Yards	7-49	10-87
Possession Time	29:23	30:37

TEXAS SHOWS 'EM

BY SUZANNE HALLIBURTON
AUSTIN AMERICAN-STATESMAN

Texas middle linebacker Aaron Harris always seemed to pick the exact gap to blitz through. He knew where Missouri quarterback Brad Smith was throwing, he anticipated the option pitches, the trick plays, every nuance that had made the Tigers offense one of the most difficult to defend —until Saturday.

It was almost as if the Longhorn senior guessed the plays before Missouri signaled them in.

"I did," Harris said afterward, without a hint of arrogance.

Led by Harris' early interception and eight tackles, the Longhorns' defense sliced apart the Tigers' offense, which had been averaging more than 550 yards and 44 points a game before encountering Texas to open Big 12 Conference play.

The major plotline of the second-ranked Longhorns' 51-20 victory Saturday was how Texas controlled the dynamic Smith, who had drawn favorable comparisons to Texas' Vince Young.

The Tigers (2-2) generated 330 yards against undefeated Texas and put up a late touchdown with 3:54 to play to bring the Longhorns' margin of victory to a misleading 31 points.

It wasn't that close, especially given that Texas helped Missouri's fortunes with an uncharacteristic 14 penalties for 135 yards, four fumbles, an interception and a failed fourth-down conversion. The Longhorns also scored their first three touchdowns on one-play drives following Missouri turnovers.

"Too many penalties, we turned it over, and we still scored 51 points," said Texas coach Mack Brown, whose Longhorns won their 11th straight game, the second longest streak in the country.

Meanwhile, the game's sub-plot was how Young shook off some early woes to overwhelm the Tigers.

Young had his best rushing performance of the season, running for 108 yards, including a 34-yard, ad-libbed scramble to convert a third-and-30 late in the second quarter when the game still was competitive. On the play, Missouri rushed only three linemen and sent eight players into coverage. Young looked deep to Ramonce Taylor, then tight end David Thomas before searching for his third outlet, tailback Selvin Young. Only then did he take off running.

OPPOSITE PAGE: **Linebacker Aaron Harris races downfield after intercepting Missouri quarterback Brad Smith's pass in the first quarter. Harris took the ball to the three-yard line on the play.** *Deborah Cannon/American-Statesman*

Young also befuddled the Missouri defense with a 33-yard scoring scamper off a fake handoff to Selvin Young in what proved to be the winning touchdown with 6:29 remaining in the first quarter.

The Longhorns' rushing attack generated 349 yards, 52 more than their average. Jamaal Charles ran for 97 yards and a touchdown, while fellow freshman Henry Melton added 57 yards with two scores.

Texas also welcomed Selvin Young, the former starter, back to the lineup, after the junior missed the previous six quarters because of a lingering ankle sprain. He ran for 65 yards on 11 carries and threw a freeing block for Vince Young, his best friend, on the 34-yard, third-down scramble.

"I feel great," said a beaming Selvin Young, who celebrated his 22nd birthday Saturday.

Vince Young, who jammed a finger and dropped three snaps early in the game, was throwing as effortlessly as he was running, completing 15 of 22 passes for 236 yards and two touchdowns.

He had a 32-yarder to an off-balance Charles and a 27-yard screen to Taylor, who made a one-handed catch and then streaked down the sideline.

OPPOSITE PAGE: Texas quarterback Vince Young unleashes a pass. Young completed 15 of 22 passes for 236 yards and two touchdowns.
Deborah Cannon/American-Statesman

BELOW: The Missouri defense closes in on Henry Melton in the fourth quarter. Melton scored two touchdowns on nine carries.
Deborah Cannon/American-Statesman

ABOVE: Senior defensive tackle Larry Dibbles comes in from the side to sack Missouri quarterback Brad Smith during the third quarter.

Deborah Cannon/American-Statesman

Aaron Ross completed the Texas scoring by returning a punt 88 yards, the third-longest in program history.

Harris' interception, which set up Charles' initial touchdown, made the first of many big Longhorns defensive plays.

It took Texas until late in the first quarter to adjust to Missouri's offense, a run-oriented attack that widened running lanes by rushing from a four-receiver set.

The Texas defensive line was called for three offsides penalties in the opening five minutes of the game. The penalties helped Missouri extend an 11-play, 87-yard scoring drive on the Tigers' second possession of the game.

Missouri's offensive line takes larger than normal splits to widen holes in the opposing defenses and open broader running lanes for Smith. In addition, the Tigers used four to five receivers for most every play, although Smith often ran from the formation.

Defensive coordinator Gene Chizik opted to keep all three of his linebackers in the game, rather than substituting for a fifth defensive back. He sent Harris on blitzes and used safeties Michael Huff and Michael Griffin to harass Smith in the backfield. Meanwhile, ends Tim Crowder and Brian Robison maintained pressure from the outside. The constant pressure finally forced Missouri's guards and tackles to line up closer together to protect Smith.

It didn't work.

Smith, who had been averaging 113 yards a game, ran 25 times but netted only 57 yards. He was sacked four times for 23 yards in losses. He completed only 19 of 37 passes for 181 yards. And he accounted for all three of Missouri's turnovers—two fumbles and an interception.

Smith "is really good, and he's so smooth," Brown said. "Sometimes he's like Vince; he doesn't look like he's running and just makes plays, but he can throw the ball, too. If you sit back and let him sit back there. . . they were just killing us to a slow death for a while until we started bringing pressure."

	1st	2nd	3rd	4th	Final
Texas	14	10	13	14	51
Missouri	13	0	0	7	20

Scoring Summary

1st- **Texas** Charles 3-yard run (Pino kick)—1 play, 3 yards in 0:03.

Missouri Jackson 12-yard run (Crossett kick)—11 plays, 87 yards in 3:41.

Texas V. Young 33-yard run (Pino kick)—1 play, 33 yards in 0:07.

Missouri Smith 3-yard run (Crossett kick failed)—13 plays, 80 yards in 5:16.

2nd-**Texas** Charles 32-yard pass from V. Young (Pino kick)—1 play, 22 yards in 0:32.

Texas Pino 26-yard field goal—14 plays, 52 yards in 4:44.

3rd- **Texas** Taylor 27-yard pass from V. Young (Pino kick)—6 plays, 80 yards in 1:10.

Texas Melton 1-yard run (Pino kick failed)—7 plays 40 yards in 2:34.

4th- **Texas** Melton 1-yard run (Pino kick)—9 plays, 55 yards in 4:42.

Texas Ross 88-yard punt return (Pino kick).

Missouri Smith 1-yard run (Crossett kick)—11 plays, 72 yards in 4:08.

Team Statistics

Category	Texas	Missouri
First Downs	23	27
Rushes-Yards (Net)	50-349	47-139
Passing Yards (Net)	236	191
Passes Att-Comp-Int	22-15-1	39-21-1
Total Offense Plays-Yards	72-585	86-330
Punt Returns-Yards	4-129	0-0
Kickoff Returns-Yards	3-74	7-120
Interception Returns-Yards	1-30	1-0
Punts (Number-Avg)	2-36.5	7-42.0
Fumbles-Lost	4-1	4-2
Sacks By (Number-Yards)	4-29	1-13
Penalties-Yards	14-135	5-31
Possession Time	29:30	30:30

SMACKED

BY SUZANNE HALLIBURTON
AUSTIN AMERICAN-STATESMAN

This was such a new feeling for the Texas football team, this giddy, postgame jubilation Saturday afternoon at the Cotton Bowl.

Quarterback Vince Young, who helped engineer the 45-12 rout of Oklahoma, could stay still only long enough for the band to play "The Eyes of Texas."

He had thrown for three touchdown passes and 241 yards but still had plenty of energy to sprint to the northwest section of the stadium and slap high-fives with everyone in burnt orange who extended a hand.

With cameras trailing him, Young ran a victory lap before curling to the 50-yard line and giving a special wave to his uncle and the rest of his family.

"I wanted them to know what I was feeling," Young said of the Longhorn fans. "They wanted to touch me, and I wanted to touch them, too."

It was chaotic all over the field as the second-ranked Longhorns celebrated their 12th consecutive win, the fifth this season.

RIGHT: The Texas defense hammers Oklahoma's Kejuan Jones during the first quarter at the SBC Red River Rivalry at the Cotton Bowl in Dallas, Texas.
Deborah Cannon/American-Statesman

Texas coach Mack Brown sought out people to hug. So did his assistants. Offensive tackle Jonathan Scott, who was standing at midfield, hoisted the coveted Golden Hat trophy over his head.

Meanwhile, Oklahoma players stayed long enough to shake hands and then plodded up the tunnel. The Sooner fans were long gone—some started leaving at the half, moments after Young found Billy Pittman for a 64-yard touchdown pass that gave the Longhorns a 24-6 lead at intermission.

Oklahoma had started the season ranked seventh in the country. After Saturday's 33-point loss, which tied OU's worst deficit in the 100 games of the series, the Sooners fell to 2-3 and 1-1 in Big 12 Conference play.

OU coach Bob Stoops appeared uncomfortable in the post game press conference as he was forced to heap unfamiliar praise on his team's biggest rival. Before Saturday, his only other loss to the Longhorns came in 1999, his first year as a head coach.

"Congratulations to Texas. They played an excellent football game," Stoops said. "The team, coaches and players really executed well and made big plays."

Thanks to those big plays, which had been lacking in the previous five meetings, Texas dominated from the first snap.

The Longhorns started the scoring on an opening, 82-yard drive that culminated in a 15-yard

BELOW: Receiver Billy Pittman's teammates pile on top of him to celebrate his second-quarter touchdown.

Deborah Cannon/American-Statesman

ABOVE: Vince Young celebrates with the fans after the Longhorns beat Oklahoma 45-12. *Jay Janner/American-Statesman*

ABOVE: **Senior linebacker Aaron Harris (2) wears the Golden Hat Trophy as his teammates look on.** *Rodolfo Gonzalez/American-Statesman*

OPPOSITE PAGE: **Defensive tackle Rodrique Wright returns a fumble by Oklahoma quarterback Rhett Bomar for a fourth-quarter touchdown.**

Jay Janner/American-Statesman

pass from Young to Ramonce Taylor. They got to the 45 when defensive tackle Rod Wright, playing in his final OU game, scooped up a fumble by OU quarterback Rhett Bomar and lumbered 67 yards to the end zone.

In between, freshman tailback Jamaal Charles took a simple zone-read handoff 80 yards—the longest run ever by a Texas back in the history of the series—to give the Longhorns a 14-6 lead. As soon as he took the handoff, Charles almost immediately broke free of the Sooner defense by faking a move to his right, then slicing left and stepping out of the grasp of three would-be tacklers. He ended the game with 116 yards.

Offensive coordinator Greg Davis used two new plays—including one that wasn't even in Saturday's game plan—that helped his unit generate 444 yards. His offense scored 38 more points and generated nearly twice as many yards as in last year's 12-0 loss to Oklahoma.

The first tweak in the plan came early, on a fourth-down sweep by Charles. OU's defense thought it would be a sneak. Instead, Charles ran around right end for an 11-yard gain that propelled the Longhorns to their first score.

The second change was on the first of two touchdown tosses from Young to Pittman. Davis knew that Oklahoma's secondary gambled, jumping

routes to be in better position for momentum-changing big hits and interceptions. Davis sent in a play the Longhorns last practiced in August—a wheel route that allowed Young three options. Young sprinted to the left, while Pittman lured safety Reggie Smith to bite on the fake. Pittman's move gave him a 10-yard cushion on Smith and an open path to the end zone.

"I'm feeling much more adventurous as Vince has matured," Davis said of Young, who is relying more on his arm and less on his graceful legs to win.

Throughout the afternoon, the defense morphed from its 4-3 base into a new look with three down linemen, two linebackers and six defensive backs. Defensive coordinator Gene Chizik tried out the new defense—Texas hasn't used such a formation in three seasons—in order to confuse Bomar, the redshirt freshman.

Bomar was made vulnerable because of an ankle injury to OU running back Adrian Peterson. Peterson did not start and carried the ball only three times for 10 yards. That performance was in sharp contrast to the 225-yard outing he turned in a year ago here.

Bomar completed 12 of his 33 passes for 94 yards. His two turnovers—Wright's fumble recovery and Michael Huff's interception—led to 14 Texas points. The Longhorn defense sacked him three times and did not let up until linebacker Rashad Bobino threw Bomar down with 2:54 to play.

Wright's reaction to his touchdown summed up the Longhorns' emotions in a handful of words.

"I was in denial the whole time I was running, the whole time I was celebrating," Wright said.

"It started to sink in after we won. But the whole time, it felt like it was unreal. . . . It's a great feeling."

	1st	2nd	3rd	4th	Final
Oklahoma	6	0	0	6	12
Texas	14	10	7	14	45

Scoring Summary

1st— **Texas** Taylor 15-yard pass from V. Young (Pino kick)—12 plays, 82 yards in 5:56.
Oklahoma Hartley 52-yard field goal—6 plays, 13 yards in 1:50.
Oklahoma Hartley 26-yard field goal—6 plays, 17 yards in 2:40.
Texas Charles 80-yard run (Pino kick)—1 play, 80 yards in 0:13.
2nd—**Texas** Pino 37-yard field goal—8 plays, 32 yards in 3:08.
Texas Pittman 64-yard pass from V. Young (Pino kick)—2 plays, 70 yards in 0:38.
3rd—**Texas** Pittman 27-yard pass from V. Young (Pino kick)—6 plays, 53 yards in 2:28.
4th—**Texas** S. Young 5-yard run (Pino kick)—10 plays, 64 yards in 3:34.
Oklahoma Finley 15-yard pass from Bomar (Bomar pass failed)—5 plays, 38 yards in 1:22.
Texas Wright 67-yard fumble recovery (Pino kick).

Team Statistics

Category	Oklahoma	Texas
First Downs	12	20
Rushes-Yards (net)	33-77	40-203
Passing Yards (net)	94	241
Passes Att-Comp-Int	33-12-1	27-14-0
Total Offense Plays-Yards	66-171	67-444
Punt Returns-Yards	1-5	2-6
Kickoff Returns-Yards	8-126	1-18
Interception Returns-Yards	0-0	1-0
Punts (Number-Avg)	7-39.9	5-37.0
Fumbles-Lost	1-1	3-1
Sacks By (Number-Yards)	3-14	3-21
Penalties-Yards	6-50	12-110
Possession Time	29:41	30:19

OPPOSITE PAGE: Billy Pittman flashes a number one as he sprints into the end zone. Pittman had four receptions for 100 yards and scored two touchdowns against Oklahoma.
Deborah Cannon/American-Statesman

PITTMAN PERSEVERES

BY CEDRIC GOLDEN, AUSTIN AMERICAN-STATESMAN

OCTOBER 12, 2005

Gwen Kelley won $1.5 million in the Texas Two-Step lottery drawing three years ago, but that luck did not immediately spread to her grandson.

Billy Pittman, one of Kelley's 21 grandchildren, was one of the best football players to come out of Yoe High School in Cameron, but his career at the University of Texas nearly ended before it started.

First it was a quadriceps injury and a bout with Bell's palsy in his freshman year. Then he hurt his other quadricep and injured his shoulder in a scrimmage as a redshirt freshman.

"I told him we don't quit in this family," said Kelley, who lives in Cameron and watches Texas' games on television. "I told him education was the number-one priority and that quitting something he loved would just hurt him later."

Long before his 63-yard catch-and-run at Ohio State or his two touchdown grabs against Oklahoma last week, Pittman was seriously considering leaving the game he had played for as long as he could remember. "It was one thing after another. It would have been easy for me to quit," said Pittman, who was hotly pursued by Nebraska as an option quarterback after an all-state senior season at Yoe. "I'm glad I didn't. It feels good to be out there because it was really tough to watch last year."

"I told him to hang in there," said Texas wide receiver Ramonce Taylor, Pittman's former youth league basketball teammate in Temple. "You could tell he was frustrated."

The biggest frustration for Pittman came one morning when his eye began twitching uncontrollably. A doctor later told him he had developed Bell's palsy, a non-fatal condition that results in weakness or paralysis on one side of the face.

"She told me I may not ever be able to move one side of my face," he said. "That was pretty scary."

Pittman said the condition lasted about a month, and he resolved to enter his sophomore season with a clean mind. He got the early attention of quarterback Vince Young in June during voluntary workouts, and the latter spoke with coach Mack Brown and offensive coordinator Greg Davis about Pittman's performances in the 7-on-7 passing scrimmages.

"I didn't know he was that fast at first," Young said. "After watching him move around against our defense, I called Coach Davis and told him, 'Billy P. is going to be good.'"

Davis calls Pittman one of the team's most precise route runners and believes the time Pittman spent in practice—the former high school quarterback served as the Longhorns' scout team

ABOVE: There's no quit in Billy Pittman, who has overcome several injuries and Bell's palsy to become one of Texas' premier receivers.

Deborah Cannon/American Statesman

QB his freshman year—has helped him mature into a good football player.

After a solid summer that saw him emerge as one of six receivers on Davis' potential list of starters, Pittman did not catch a pass in the opener against Louisiana-Lafayette, but he made a huge impression at Ohio State with five catches for 130 yards and his first touchdown.

Last week before a national television audience, he erased any chance of sneaking up on future opponents with four catches for 100 yards, including a 64-yard scoring reception in the final minute of the first half. He also made a one-handed, 27-yard TD grab in the third quarter despite being held by an OU defender.

"He was cheating," Pittman said, smiling.

Pittman's speed has helped the Texas offense take flight during the first half the season. He's second on the team with 13 receptions and is tops in receiving yardage (311 yards) and yards per catch (23.4). And his emancipation from the injury bug has admittedly left him with thicker skin.

And his teammates have tested that thicker skin.

He was teased for being run down by Ohio State's Tyler Everett on the aforementioned 63-yard pass. Then two weeks ago, he lost his balance inside the Missouri 5-yard line after hauling in a 41-yard pass from Young.

Longhorns free safety Michael Griffin said Monday that Pittman has the unique ability to trip over a blade of grass. Minutes later, Tarell Brown's cell phone rang and it was Pittman, who playfully hung up after Brown told him Griffin was having fun at his expense.

Pittman is finally able to smile after a tumultuous start to his college career. "After all I've been through, it's good to know the hard work is finally starting to pay off," he said.

And Grandma is already making plans for the New Year.

"I've never seen him play a college game in person," she said. "I would love to see him play in the Rose Bowl."

> "After all I've been through, it's good to know the hard work is finally starting to pay off."
>
> –Billy Pittman, Longhorn receiver

ABOVE: Against Oklahoma, Pittman caught four passes for 100 yards and scored twice. *Jay Janner/American-Statesman*

YOUNG AT HEART

BY SUZANNE HALLIBURTON
AUSTIN AMERICAN-STATESMAN

The Colorado defense gambled to open its game against Texas Saturday afternoon. The Buffaloes, knowing that the Longhorns were the second-best rushing team in the country, moved their safeties closer to the line to clog any running lanes that possibly could be created.

They figured that Vince Young, the most gifted running quarterback in the country, couldn't beat them with his arm.

Bad move. Call Colorado's gamble snake eyes on a football field.

In leading the Longhorns to a 42-17 manhandling of the 24th-ranked Buffaloes, Young became the most accurate single-game passer in program history.

Young attempted 29 throws on a sun-splashed afternoon at Royal-Memorial Stadium. He completed 25 of them to seven different receivers for a collective 336 yards and two touchdowns—his first 300-yard passing game.

And as Colorado expected, Young did run the ball, gaining 58 yards and scoring three touchdowns, all in the first half as Texas built a 35-0 lead by intermission.

"Vince's performance today was the best I've ever seen him," said Texas coach Mack Brown.

"They weren't going to allow us to run the ball, which was fine."

The only disappointment No. 2 Texas (6-0, 3-0 in Big 12) experienced came after the game, when the players grouped around three televisions in the locker room to watch the last few seconds of top-ranked Southern California's come-from-behind, 34-31 victory over Notre Dame. The Longhorns, though, were content with extending their winning streak to 13 games, including seven straight over ranked teams, as they now gear up for next Saturday's game against 13th-ranked Texas Tech.

The Texas defense dismantled Colorado's offense, which relies heavily on the runs of Hugh Charles to set up Joel Klatt's play-action passes.

By the second half, Buffaloes coach Gary Barnett junked his game plan of balanced, power football. Charles, the third-leading rusher in the Big 12, carried 13 times for 38 yards. Klatt, who amassed 398 yards throwing a week ago against Texas A&M, managed a pedestrian 189 yards against the Longhorns. Klatt completed 78 percent of his passes against the Aggies but struggled mightily against the Longhorns, completing 49 percent.

OPPOSITE PAGE: Quarterback Vince Young gets away from Colorado's Jordon Dizon during the second quarter. Young ran for three touchdowns against Colorado. *Deborah Cannon/American-Statesman*

The Longhorns blitzed their linebackers and safeties early, then relied on their defensive line to rush Klatt in the second half.

"Our whole objective was to disrupt (Klatt's) timing," said Texas defensive coordinator Gene Chizik. "As the game went on, we got good pressure."

Behind Young—the undisputed star of the game —Texas did not need to punt until the third quarter. By then, the Longhorns had scored touchdowns on their first five drives, missing an opportunity on a sixth when David Pino's 39-yard field goal attempt drifted wide right.

	1st	2nd	3rd	4th	Final
Colorado	0	10	0	7	17
Texas	14	21	0	7	42

Scoring Summary

1st— **Texas** V. Young 1-yard run (Pino kick)—16 plays, 90 yards in 7:40.

Texas V. Young 16-yard run (Pino kick)—6 plays, 67 yards in 3:05.

2nd— **Texas** S. Young 5-yard run (Pino kick)—4 plays, 75 yards in 1:52.

Texas V. Young 9-yard run (Pino kick)—8 plays, 37 yards in 3:14.

Colorado Crosby 48-yard field goal—11 plays, 47 yards in 2:54.

Texas Sweed 35-yard pass from V. Young (Pino kick)—5 plays, 72 yards in 1:31.

Colorado Judge 8-yard pass from Klatt (Crosby kick)—8 plays, 64 yards in 1:38.

4th— **Texas** Sweed 13-yard pass from V. Young (Pino kick)—9 plays, 49 yards in 4:10.

Colorado Klopfenstein 4-yard pass from Klatt (Crosby kick)—4 plays, 5 yards in 0:52.

Team Statistics

Category	Colorado	Texas
First Downs	14	24
Rushes-Yards (net)	19-45	47-145
Passing Yards (net)	192	337
Passes Att-Comp-Int	44-21-1	32-26-0
Total Offense Plays-Yards	63-237	79-482
Punt Returns-Yards	2-6	4-24
Kickoff Returns-Yards	5-89	2-51
Interception Returns-Yards	0-0	1-5
Punts (Number-Avg)	7-40.1	3-39.7
Fumbles-Lost	2-1	2-1
Sacks By (Number-Yards)	0-0	0-0
Penalties-Yards	11-83	8-70
Possession Time	21:06	38:54

"Today, Vince Young was one heck of a football player," said Barnett, whose team dropped to 4-2 and 2-1 in league play. "Everybody on our team has a great deal of respect for him. . . . The Texas offensive line did a great job of protecting Vince. He had plenty of time in the pocket, and we did not have much of a pass rush today."

Young said he and offensive coordinator Greg Davis talked about Colorado's zone defense all week, how the Buffaloes rarely allowed a big play and how they devoted most of their personnel into taking away the run and making a team one-dimensional.

Davis instructed Young to be patient, to pick his spots. There would be breakdowns in the zones, if Young could throw deep over the secondary or find tight end David Thomas on short routes he could "manufacture" into significant gains.

"Coach Davis told me to take what they give you," Young said. "Whatever it takes to win the ball game. I don't care if I have to run it 100 times or pass it 100 times, whatever it takes to win."

A year ago, Young likely wouldn't have been so patient, relying on his legs to beat a defense. "The truth is, this was the maturation of a quarterback," Davis said.

Young was impressive on all his throws. Perhaps his most memorable completion came early in the second quarter when he stayed deliberate in the pocket, waiting for a receiver to break free. He threw across his body deep to Billy Pittman, who ran underneath the throw for a 62-yard gain. It was Young's second 60-plus-yard completion to Pittman in as many games.

Limas Sweed, with seven catches for 88 yards and two touchdowns, was Young's favorite Saturday. Thomas helped him crush Colorado's zone five times for 64 yards. With the safeties cheating to play the run, Thomas was open on most any play.

OPPOSITE PAGE: Billy Pittman splits Colorado defenders J.J. Billingsley and Abraham Wright during the second quarter. Pittman and quarterback Vince Young connected on three passes for 99 yards.
Deborah Cannon/American-Statesman

ABOVE: Vince Young (10) goes over the top with the help of junior guard Kasey Studdard (64) to score against Colorado.
Matt Rourke/American-Statesman

OPPOSITE PAGE: Limas Sweed celebrates his 35-yard touchdown catch in the second quarter.
Sweed made seven receptions for 88 yards and two touchdowns. *Deborah Cannon/American-Statesman*

Young's arm became even more important in the game plan when it became clear that the ankle of freshman darter Jamaal Charles would allow him to do nothing more than run straight ahead.

Charles, the starter for the past three games, carried the ball three times, all in one series. He then took a seat on the bench, leaving Selvin Young the chore of trying to penetrate Colorado's formidable defense, which often used nine men gathered near the line of scrimmage.

The strategy has been good for the Buffaloes all season, limiting offenses to 77 yards rushing a game. Texas gained 145 and was happy with that total.

"We didn't want to be stubborn," Brown said. "We rushed for 145. We'll take that."

GAME 7: **TEXAS 52** TEXAS TECH 17

October 22, 2005
Darrell K Royal–Texas Memorial Stadium
Austin, Texas

TECH WRECKED

BY SUZANNE HALLIBURTON
AUSTIN AMERICAN-STATESMAN

Members of the Texas defense were gimpy Saturday evening, limping about the locker room, trying to catch their breath.

It was nice to celebrate a 52-17 manhandling of 10th-ranked Texas Tech, but the most popular place after the game was the training room where they stash the tape and the ice.

The Longhorns' defense was on the field at Royal-Memorial Stadium for an energy-sapping 93 snaps. Tech gained 468 yards and kept the ball for an intimidating 36 minutes.

Yet it was all according to plan.

"It's always about the points," said Texas defensive coordinator Gene Chizik.

So given Chizik's logic, the last significant play the Longhorns gave up came with 8:39 to go in the third quarter, when Cody Hodges, the nation's most prolific passer, threw a 6-yard touchdown pass to Joel Filani. It was the last time Tech scored, cutting the Longhorns' lead to 21 points.

RIGHT: Texas Tech's Taurean Henderson falls victim to the UT defense of Robert Killebrew (40), Larry Dibbles (92), and Aaron Harris.
Deborah Cannon/American-Statesman

The victory allowed the Longhorns to stretch their winning streak to 14 games. The outcome tied the school record for most lopsided victory over a top 10 team. The only game that was as dominant was back in 1970, when the Longhorns knocked off fourth-ranked Arkansas 42-7 to clinch the program's last national championship.

Texas appears to be on a similar path this season. Two members of the Rose Bowl selection committee—their game hosts the national championship Jan. 4—greeted the Longhorns in the locker room after the game.

When the Bowl Championship Series rankings are announced Monday, it's a given that the Tech victory will strengthen Texas' hold on the No. 2 spot. Tech (6-1, 3-1) had been seventh best in the BCS last week.

"This team continues to impress us as a staff," said Texas coach Mack Brown. "Our guys were excited about this game, but we are still a work in progress. We have the ability to play much better. . . If you don't play your best game, and you still are able to score 52 points, you know you have a special team out there."

ABOVE: Texas' Ramonce Taylor avoids a tackle by Tech's John Saldi. *Kelly West/American-Statesman*

OPPOSITE PAGE: Robert Killebrew (40) and Nick Schroeder (53) flatten Texas Tech punt returner Danny Amendola in the third quarter. *Brian K. Diggs/American-Statesman*

The Texas defense proved to be the story on a day when normally spectacular quarterback Vince Young was sub par.

"I'd give myself a C-plus," Young said.

He was 12 of 22 for 239 yards, with two touchdowns to Billy Pittman. Young flashed a Heisman pose after the second scoring strike in the third quarter. He also rushed for 45 yards and another score. But his two first-quarter interceptions on consecutive drives kept the game competitive—Tech actually led 7-3, then tied the game at 10 with 11:11 remaining before halftime.

At 10-10, Texas exploded for three consecutive touchdowns, kicked off by Selvin Young's 10-yard dash to give the Longhorns a lead they didn't relinquish. The next two scores were set up by the defense and special teams.

Safety Michael Griffin, who was anticipating a fake, tackled punter Alex Reyes and got a hand on the kick, giving the Longhorns possession at the

BELOW: Texas running back Selvin Young scores a touchdown in the second quarter. Young had 16 carries for 77 yards and two touchdowns.
Deborah Cannon/American-Statesman

Tech 23. Texas took two plays to score, with Young rolling to his left and finding Pittman for the 15-yard touchdown.

Tech then began a methodical march downfield. On the 10th play of the drive and poised at the Texas 7, Hodges was no match for the rush from Texas' four-man line. Texas was anticipating a short pass. Middle linebacker Aaron Harris had a pass bounce off his helmet. Defensive end Tim Crowder caught the deflection with one hand.

Helped greatly by a 48-yard completion to Pittman, the Longhorns upped the margin to 31-10 on Selvin Young's second touchdown.

If compared to the average, balanced offense in college football, Hodges' numbers were impressive. He completed 42 of 64 passes for 369 yards and two touchdowns. However, they were far below his season average of 410 passing yards a game.

Tech had 307 total yards through two quarters, but the Texas defense limited the Raiders to 137 in the second half.

Chizik and co-coordinator Duane Akina had the Longhorns rely on man coverage about 80 percent of the game. They morphed their fronts, using four down linemen, then three. On second and third downs, Texas almost always relied on a dime, or six defensive back, package. They wanted to limit Tech's passing to short dinks while shutting down the long bombs. Of the 64 attempts, only four were long balls.

The alignment of Tech's offensive line also was a problem. They take significant splits, with 6 feet separating the guards from the tackles. These splits literally take the opposing defensive ends out of the game plan, since the ends often are lining up 10 yards from the quarterback they're trying to sack.

But Brian Robison and Crowder, the Texas ends, still managed to dominate. Robison had three sacks. Crowder had one sack and the interception.

The two combined on what could have been another touchdown late in the game, when Robison sacked Hodges and appeared to strip the ball from the quarterback. But Crowder's route to the end zone was interrupted by an early whistle. Officials ruled that Hodges was down, a call that drew loud boos for several minutes from the crowd of 83,919.

After the game, Robison was asked if he was going out to celebrate the victory. Or if he'd rather go to bed.

He thought about party versus an early bedtime, then shook his head.

"I don't know," Robison said. "It depends on how I feel when I leave here."

	1st	2nd	3rd	4th	Final
Texas Tech	7	3	7	0	17
Texas	10	21	14	7	52

Scoring Summary

1st— **Texas** Pino 40-yard field goal—6 plays, 21 yards in 2:24.

Texas Tech Henderson 3-yard pass from Hodges (Trlica kick)—4 plays, 21 yards in 1:48.

Texas Melton 1-yard run (Pino kick)—3 plays, eight yards in 1:23.

2nd— **Texas Tech** Trlica 32-yard field goal—14 plays, 65 yards in 5:01.

Texas S. Young 10-yard run (Pino kick)—7 plays, 80 yards in 2:13.

Texas Pittman 15-yard pass from V. Young (Pino kick)—2 plays, 23 yards in 0:11.

Texas S. Young 7-yard run (Pino kick)—4 plays, 88 yards in 0:49.

3rd— **Texas** Pittman 75-yard pass from V. Young (Pino kick)—3 plays, 80 yards in 1:18.

Texas Tech Filani 6-yard pass from Hodges (Trlica kick)—15 plays, 80 yards in 5:03.

Texas V. Young 10-yard run (Pino kick)—11 plays, 65 yards in 4:24.

4th— **Texas** Ogbonnaya 22-yard run (Pino kick)—2 plays, 26 yards in 0:51.

Team Statistics

Category	TEXAS TECH	TEXAS
First Downs	29	21
Rushes-Yards (Net)	29-99	40-205
Passing Yards (Net)	369	239
Passes Att-Comp-Int	64-42-1	22-12-2
Total Offense Plays-Yards	93-468	62-444
Fumble Returns-Yards	0-0	0-0
Punt Returns-Yards	1-6	5-123
Kickoff Returns-Yards	5-88	2-67
Interception Returns-Yards	2-39	1-0
Punts (Number-Avg)	7-33.4	3-36.7
Fumbles-Lost	1-1	1-0
Sacks By (Number-Yards)	0-0	6-51
Penalties-Yards	10-78	3-35
Possession Time	36:01	23:59

MIDDLE GROUND FITS HARRIS BEST

BY CEDRIC GOLDEN, *AUSTIN AMERICAN-STATESMAN*

OCTOBER 28, 2005

During an interview, Aaron Harris sometimes pauses between words to carefully sculpt his thoughts, as if he is hesitant to blurt out something he may regret.

The Texas senior linebacker shows none of that reserve on the football field, where he is a 230-pound ball of fury seeking contact, any contact, as he bounces into blockers and ball-carriers. Harris is the one co-defensive coordinator Gene Chizik mentions to his freshmen as the type of player he wants on the Texas defense. Smart. Relentless. Violent.

"He's been huge for us in the locker room," Chizik said. "Aaron Harris comes to work prepared, he studies film, works hard, puts it all on the line every day. He's the perfect example of what a defensive player should be."

The hard-hitting Harris burst upon the Big 12 scene last season with 18 tackles in a loss to Oklahoma and has finally emerged from the shadow of departed All-American Derrick Johnson. Harris ranks first among the Longhorns in solo tackles and second in sacks, registering 3 1/2. He's also forced two fumbles and intercepted a pass.

The big hitter on a fast Texas defense, he is a tireless pursuer. On Saturday in the Longhorns' 52-17 rout of Texas Tech, he received fluids intravenously after becoming dehydrated but continued to play, even though Texas coach Mack Brown offered him a spot on the bench with the game well in hand.

"He is deserving of All-America consideration," Brown said. "Aaron is having that type of season."

Before he became a Butkus Award candidate, Harris struggled to find middle ground between his on-field aggression and his off-the-field existence. The lessons he learned haven't all come easily.

In May of 2004, Harris and a teammate, Eric Hall, were attacked by a group of men outside a Sixth Street business. Each player suffered a broken jaw and had to undergo surgery, which resulted in the two men having their jaws wired shut. Harris lost 20 pounds as a result.

One year earlier, Harris and three teammates were arrested and charged with marijuana possession after a traffic stop in Madison County in East Texas. The charges were later dropped when it was discovered the drugs found in the vehicle belonged to someone else.

The incidents have taught Harris to be more careful about his surroundings and choices. Anthony Harris, who himself was attacked and knocked unconscious as a sixth-grader living in Dallas, counseled his son to be more aware and to think before acting.

ABOVE: Texas' Aaron Harris (2) tackles Texas A&M's Jorvorskie Lane in College Station.

Deborah Cannon/American-Statesman

Aaron Harris listened. "It was me being in bad places at bad times and making bad choices," said Harris, 21. "Now I know my choices can affect my life and my family. I stay home and shoot pool now because there are situations out there that make you think about the consequences."

For Harris and his parents, it was Mack Brown's friendly demeanor and belief in family that made Texas the choice over Oklahoma and Texas A&M when Harris was being recruited out of North Mesquite High. Tina Harris, an assistant high school principal, is from Ardmore, Okla., and her

BEYOND Xs AND Os

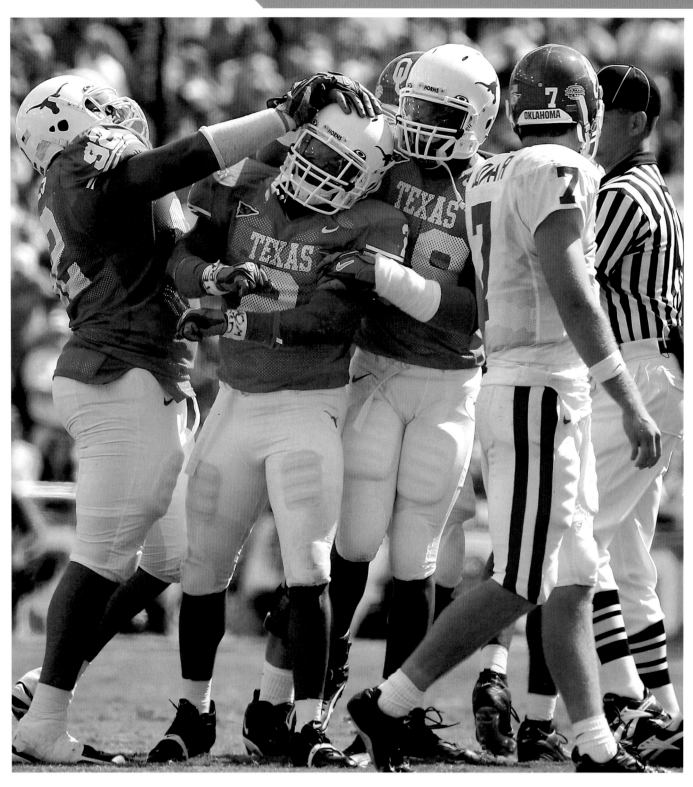

ABOVE: Aaron Harris (2) is congratulated by teammates Larry Dibbles (92) and Brian Orakpo (98) during a game against Oklahoma. *Deborah Cannon/American-Statesman*

ties to the Sooner State made the decision much more difficult. Still, the family liked Austin and the educational opportunities offered by UT.

"I major in youth community studies and plan to get a teaching certificate," Harris said.

"My parents said I was going to Texas to get a degree. The football was going to be there, but graduating was more important."

Since his arrival at Texas, it's been Harris' M.O. to take on challenges head-on, a trait that was evident from the first day he donned a Texas jersey. He remembers one challenge in particular: Will Matthews.

Harris roomed with Matthews, the Texas fullback, during his freshman year, and one night, friendly banter about the next day's full-contact drills turned into a little trash-talking session about who would get the better of the other.

It turned out to be Harris who finished as the runner-up after suffering a concussion when he and the 250-pound Matthews collided, helmet-to-helmet, in a scrimmage. Harris was knocked out cold and was rushed to the hospital.

"My wife got in the ambulance, and I was going to follow behind them but first I heard this knock on my window," said Anthony Harris. "It was Sally Brown. She rode with me to the hospital and she and Coach Brown stayed with us until Aaron was released. For parents who had just sent their baby off to college, that let us know we had made the right choice."

"I was still going to be relentless after that," Aaron Harris said. "Nothing changed."

But Harris has. He once looked to Johnson, a first-round NFL draft pick in April, for advice. Now younger Longhorns players, such as redshirt freshman Rashad Bobino and sophomore Robert Killebrew, pelt him with questions daily. And not all of the queries are about football.

"We talked about his past experiences during two-a-days," said Bobino, who calls Harris his big brother. "He told me he didn't want me to take the hard road like he did. I've learned a lot from him."

Harris comes from a family of football players, but none but him played defense. Anthony Harris was a wide receiver at South Oak Cliff while his other sons, Antony and Justin, played tailback and wide receiver at North Mesquite High. Aaron Harris scored on a long touchdown run the first time he touched the ball as a fullback in pee wee play. And he hated it.

"Aaron always wanted to be a linebacker," said childhood friend Tarell Brown, a Longhorns teammate who also played in that pee wee game. "He always wanted to hit somebody and didn't like getting hit."

By the start of high school, Harris was a fullback/linebacker, but conversations with North Mesquite alums Brian Hickman and Josh Buhl (who went on to star at Kansas State) persuaded him to become a full-time linebacker by his junior year in high school.

As a senior, Harris was named his district's defensive MVP. He earned the nickname of the "Human Tackling Machine" after registering 188 stops despite playing only nine games because of an ankle injury.

Harris is listed at 6 feet and 230 pounds, but is probably closer to 5-10. As the NFL beckons, he is not deterred by talk of him being too short to play linebacker in the pros. He's roughly the same size as NFL All-Pros Zach Thomas and London Fletcher. Another guy his size, Mike Singletary, made it to the Pro Football Hall of Fame.

"I still have something to prove," Harris said. "They say I'm too short, that I'm too slow. I heard it all growing up and I hear it now. I take it all as fuel."

October 29, 2005
Boone Pickens Stadium
Stillwater, Oklahoma

GREAT ESCAPE

BY SUZANNE HALLIBURTON
AUSTIN AMERICAN-STATESMAN

N o one flinched on the Texas sideline Saturday night as Oklahoma State, possibly the worst team in the Big 12 Conference, built a 19-point advantage in the first half.

The Cowboys took advantage of Longhorn turnovers, of drive-stalling penalties. They even used a weird bounce to complete a 29-yard touchdown pass near the end of the second quarter to go up 28-9.

It all better served to build the suspense of an eventual 47-28 UT victory and add a chapter to the ever-growing legend of Texas quarterback Vince Young.

"Whatever it took," a smiling and very relaxed Young said after the game.

What it took was Young's poise under pressure. The Longhorns needed Young to run for 267 yards and two touchdowns, including an 80-yard scramble three plays into the third quarter. He also needed to throw for 239 yards and a pair of scores.

RIGHT: Quarterback Vince Young cuts through the Oklahoma State defense in the first half at Boone Pickens Stadium in Stillwater.
Brian K. Diggs/American-Statesman

On Young's final play of the game, a 13-yard slide near the Oklahoma State sideline, he reached 506 yards in total offense, breaking the school record of 476 that had been owned by Major Applewhite.

Young also became the seventh quarterback in NCAA history to rush for 200 and throw for 200 in a single game.

But possibly most important to Texas' national championship dreams, Young directed his eighth career second-half comeback.

"When Vince steps up, everybody steps up," said Texas coach Mack Brown.

The game was weirdly similar to last year's Oklahoma State game in Austin, when Young set a then-school record in passing efficiency to erase a 28-point Cowboy advantage.

Saturday's recovery from 19 points down was only the second-biggest comeback in program history, but given that it saved the Longhorns' national championship hopes, it probably will go down as the most memorable.

Texas will find out Monday whether it remains as the top-ranked team in the Bowl Championship Series standings. No doubt, there will be some tightening in the rankings, after Southern

ABOVE: Ramonce Taylor greets Texas fans after the Longhorns defeated the Cowboys 47-28. *Brian K. Diggs/American-Statesman*

OPPOSITE PAGE: Texas tight end David Thomas (16) pulls in a catch for a first-quarter touchdown. Thomas had six receptions for 104 yards against OSU. *Brian K. Diggs/American-Statesman*

California beat up Washington State 55-13 and No. 3 Virginia Tech knocked off No. 13 Boston College 30-10.

"I'm not saying we were big-headed," said Texas receiver/tailback Ramonce Taylor. "But this was good just to calm us down a little bit, since we were No. 1 in the BCS."

Young and company officially saved the season with 48 seconds remaining in the third quarter. It

	1st	2nd	3rd	4th	Final
Texas	9	3	22	13	47
OK State	**21**	**7**	**0**	**0**	**28**

Scoring Summary

1st– **Ok. State** Woods 49-yard pass from Pena (Redden kick)–4 plays, 58 yards in 2:02.

Texas Thomas 20-yard pass from V. Young (Pino kick blocked)–11 plays, 62 yards in 3:37.

Ok. State Crosslin 4-yard run (Redden kick)–9 plays, 76 yards in 3:18.

Ok. State Pena 17-yard run (Redden kick)–1 play, 17 yards in 0:05.

Texas Pino 45-yard field goal–6 plays, 52 yards in 1:06.

2nd– **Ok. State** Woods 29-yard pass from Pena (Redden kick)–2 plays, 29 yards in 0:09.

Texas Pino 21-yard field goal–14 plays, 35 yards in 5:44.

3rd– **Texas** V. Young 80-yard run (Pino kick)–3 plays, 80 yards in 0:52.

Texas V. Young 8-yard run (Pino kick)–10 plays, 75 yards in 3:18.

Texas Tweedie 21-yard pass from V. Young (Hall pass from V. Young)–4 plays, 59 yards in 0:25.

4th– **Texas** Taylor, Ramonce 57-yard run (V. Young pass failed)–2 plays, 63 yards in 0:50.

Texas Taylor, Ramonce 12-yard run (Pino kick)–8 plays, 58 yards in 4:41.

Team Statistics

Category	Texas	Ok. State
First downs	22	20
Rushes-Yards (Net)	49-367	46-250
Passing Yards (Net)	239	152
Passes Att-Comp-Int	31-15-1	27-12-0
Total offense plays-Yards	80-606	73-402
Fumble Returns-Yards	0-0	0-0
Punt Returns-Yards	2-23	1-32
Kickoff Returns-Yards	3-73	7-114
Interception Returns-Yards	0-0	1-21
Punts (Number-Avg)	2-38.0	7-33.4
Fumbles-Lost	1-1	1-1
Sacks By (Number-Yards)	1-15	2-9
Penalties-Yards	9-60	9-80
Possession Time	30:46	29:14

took a pass to backup tight end Neale Tweedie, known most for his blocking abilities, to score the go-ahead touchdown.

Coincidentally, it was the second time in the third quarter that the Cowboys were burned by Young and Tweedie on a play known as "R Deuce Up B Pap 999 Leak Go."

On the go-ahead touchdown, David Thomas was the primary receiver as the Longhorns went to a double tight-end formation to offset the opportunistic Oklahoma State blitz. Instead, Young found a wide-open Tweedie for the 21-yard touchdown.

He then tossed a swing pass to seldom-used fullback Ahmard Hall for the two-point conversion to go up 34-28.

Taylor added a 57-yard scamper and 12-yard run late in the fourth quarter to give Texas the final 19-point cushion.

Texas increased its winning streak to 15 games, while Oklahoma State dropped to 3-5. The game was harsh on Texas starters, with six limping off the field along with two backup running backs.

Texas needed a Herculean effort from Young and the rest of the team because the Longhorns played their most disastrous first half since this time a year ago, when the Cowboys built a four-touchdown lead in the opening two quarters.

For much of the first half Saturday, the defense had no answer for Cowboys tailback Mike Hamilton, who rushed for 114 yards on 18 carries in the half, 194 by game's end.

Oklahoma State also benefited from a miracle play for its final touchdown of the half. That's when Michael Huff deflected a pass with both hands that ended up with D'Juan Woods, the trailing receiver. Woods caught the deflection with one hand and then streaked untouched for the 29-yard touchdown. It gave Oklahoma State a 28-9 lead with 5:44 to play in the second quarter.

In the first half, the UT offense also was miserable. Young, despite running for 133 yards, turned the ball over twice, setting up 14 Cowboys points.

Holding penalties against Thomas and Jonathan Scott wiped away Longhorn touchdowns. And kicker David Pino suffered two blocks—on an extra point and 53-yard field goal attempt.

By game's end, the Longhorns more than evened the special teams score with a field-goal block and two punt deflections.

The defense stopped Oklahoma State enough in the second half to give the Longhorns time to come back and set up Young's dramatics.

"I love playing with these guys," Young said. "They keep themselves poised and they keep fighting. When we get down like we did, you do not see anyone getting rattled or thinking we are going to lose."

ABOVE: Cornerback Michael Huff (7) brings down OSU running back Mike Hamilton in the first half.

Brian K. Diggs/American-Statesman

November 5, 2005
Floyd Casey Stadium
Waco, Texas

BEARING DOWN

BY SUZANNE HALLIBURTON
AUSTIN AMERICAN-STATESMAN

All season, Texas has looked for that elusive perfect outing, the contest in which the Longhorns overwhelm an opponent on both sides of the ball, where third downs are free and easy, where chasing running backs feels as effortless as a game of touch in the back yard.

The Longhorns discovered near-perfection on a blustery Saturday afternoon at Floyd Casey Stadium:

Texas 62, Baylor 0.

The No. 2 Longhorns' ninth victory of the season and 16th in a row should be more than good enough to keep Texas among the top two in this week's Bowl Championship Series ratings and, with losses by previously undefeated No. 3 Virginia Tech and No. 7 UCLA, on a trek due west to the Rose Bowl for the national championship.

"I thought our team wanted to send a message today," said Texas coach Mack Brown, "the message being that we're one of the two best teams in the country—that hasn't been in question this year."

"Today we won by 62, without running it up."

Baylor, which took Oklahoma and Texas A&M to overtime in losses last month, dropped to 4-5. The Bears still could earn a bowl trip if they win their remaining two games against Missouri and Oklahoma State.

The Texas highlights on a day when there were many included:

• Quarterback Vince Young, who played four snaps into the fourth quarter, completing 16 of 27 passes for 298 yards and two touchdowns. He also contributed 53 yards rushing.

• Ramonce Taylor excelling with his feet and hands. He ran for 102 yards and three touchdowns. And he caught a 42-yard touchdown pass from Young early in the third quarter to push the Longhorns' lead to 34-0.

• Jamaal Charles, who rotated with Taylor at tailback, gaining 72 yards and scoring twice.

• Overall, the offense generated 645 yards, its second consecutive game of 600-yards plus. And the Longhorns remained the only team in the country to score at least 50 points in five games this season.

• The Longhorns defense, which still was stinging from the 28 first-half points it allowed a week ago against Oklahoma State, enjoying its first shutout in 20 games. Baylor limped to 201 total yards—112 on the ground and only 89 via the air.

OPPOSITE PAGE: Ramonce Taylor scores one of his four touchdowns in Texas' romp of Baylor. *Deborah Cannon/American-Statesman*

ABOVE: **Jamaal Charles protects the ball from the Baylor defense. Charles scored twice on the Bears.** *Deborah Cannon/American-Statesman*

OPPOSITE PAGE: **Baylor quarterback Terrance Parks has no chance against Texas defenders Aaron Lewis (95) , Christopher Brown (48) and Michael Griffin (27).** *Deborah Cannon/American-Statesman*

The day's most spectacular play—a 42-yard touchdown from Young to Taylor—came five snaps into the third quarter. The play was called "R Deuce Up 65 Zone Nude, Up, Special," and it was designed specifically for Taylor, the fastest player on the Longhorns' offense.

Texas has used it only twice this season. Against Colorado, Young overthrew Taylor. But on Saturday, Taylor faked a block, followed offensive tackle Jonathan Scott, then scampered to the sideline, where he had plenty of time to await Young's pass.

Taylor had at least a 15-yard cushion—the Baylor defense had assumed he would stick near Young and block.

"Texas is pretty good—there's no question about that," said Baylor coach Guy Morriss.

"We lost our composure, but that's what good football teams do to you. We knew they were good,

but I didn't think we'd get dominated like that on both sides of the ball."

Baylor briefly responded to Taylor's touchdown catch, mounting its best drive of the game. The Bears reached the Texas 12, but with a fourth-and-4, Morriss sent in the field-goal team.

However, Texas' Robert Killebrew, who was lined up in the middle, got his right hand on Ryan Haven's kick, slugging the 30-yard attempt to the far left of the end zone. It was Killebrew's third block in the past two games. Against Oklahoma State, he deflected two punts.

After the field-goal try with 9:44 to go in the third quarter, the Bears crossed the 50 only one other time, getting to the 49 with five minutes remaining in the game.

"We tried to play the game of defense the way it was supposed to be played," said Texas co-defensive coordinator Gene Chizik. "It's good to see them respond with a shutout. The timing of it was really key."

Chizik conceded that his defense was embarrassed a week ago in Stillwater, specifically for allowing Cowboys running back Mike Hamilton to gain 194 rushing yards.

On Saturday, Bears tailback Brandon Whitaker was the top rusher on his team with 49 yards. Morriss changed quarterbacks for Texas, going with the more athletic Terrance Parks, but Parks completed an anemic 10 of 23 passes. He was picked off twice.

Meantime, Texas offensive coordinator Greg Davis said he challenged his team to put together two sparkling halves, something the Longhorns hadn't done this season. Texas failed to score on two of its first three series, then reeled off eight consecutive touchdowns.

Reserve quarterback Matt Nordgren added a 29-yard TD run with 5:18 to play. He fumbled on the play, but the ball bounced back to him.

"I just think we let everybody know," said Texas defensive end Brian Orakpo, "how good we are if we play an entire game."

OPPOSITE PAGE: Quan Cosby runs for a touchdown during the third quarter after a 55-yard pass from Vince Young.
Deborah Cannon/American-Statesman

	1st	2nd	3rd	4th	Final
Texas	6	21	21	14	62
Baylor	0	0	0	0	0

Scoring Summary

1st— **Texas** Charles 4-yard run (Pino kick failed)—5 plays, 68 yards in 1:34.

2nd— **Texas** Melton 1-yard run (Pino kick)—4 plays, 32 yards in 1:40.
Texas Charles 7-yard run (Pino kick)—14 plays, 80 yards in 5:48.
Texas Taylor 9-yard run (Pino kick)—2 plays, 38 yards in 0:31.

3rd— **Texas** Taylor 42-yard pass from V. Young (Pino kick)—1 play, 42 yards in 0:09.
Texas Taylor 3-yard run (Pino kick)—13 plays, 80 yards in 5:22.
Texas Cosby 55-yard pass from V. Young (Pino kick)—4 plays, 71 yards in 1:31.

4th— **Texas** Taylor 11-yard run (Pino kick)—5 plays, 92 yards in 1:17.
Texas Nordgren 15-yard run (Pino kick)—11 plays, 67 yards in 6:28.

Team Statistics

Category	Texas	Baylor
First downs	35	13
Rushes-Yards (Net)	54-347	30-112
Passing Yards (Net)	298	89
Passes Att-Comp-Int	27-16-0	23-10-2
Total Offense Plays-Yards	81-645	53-201
Fumble Returns-Yards	0-0	0-0
Punt Returns-Yards	4-67	0-0
Kickoff Returns-Yards	0-0	6-140
Interception Returns-Yards	2-11	0-0
Punts (Number-Avg)	1-35.0	8-47.2
Fumbles-Lost	3-0	0-0
Sacks By (Number-Yards)	2-16	0-0
Penalties-Yards	8-93	10-77
Possession Time	35:27	24:33

VINCE YOUNG: A STUDY IN SUCCESS

BY KEVIN ROBBINS, AUSTIN AMERICAN-STATESMAN

NOVEMBER 6, 2005

When he looked out beyond his offensive line, Vince Young saw what he expected to see.

The Baylor linebackers were where he figured to find them. The safeties were deep, the cornerbacks wide. He could place the linemen with his eyes shut.

"That's what was in the scouting report," Young said.

The Longhorns won their 26th game Saturday with Young as their starting quarterback.

They've stacked together 16 consecutive victories, a string that includes the Rose Bowl in January, which is when Young began his campaign to become the most prepared player in college football.

He was tired of surprises. He wanted predictability. He wanted to know what a defense would do before he took a snap.

This season, Young has begun every Monday since August by taking a DVD home to watch after dinner. It's a recording of his next opponent's last game.

He watches the game to the end, then rewinds from the fourth quarter back to the first. In his mind, he puts his own team on the field and imagines how his line, tight ends, receivers and backs will react to the schemes that he sees on his screen.

Against Baylor, Young knew he would scarcely see a blitz, that the Bears would try to squelch his runs and make him throw.

He was ready. He passed for 298 yards and a pair of touchdowns. He rushed for 53 yards—an amount that might seem short of his standard.

Then again, he expected as much.

"It's indescribable," said receiver Billy Pittman, who caught three of those passes for 60 yards. "He never gets surprised."

Young and coach Mack Brown have had many conversations this year about the difference between this season and the others. They've talked about experience, poise, grace, composure and what it takes to become the kind of player teammates will trust no matter how far behind they are and how much time is left.

"What he's saying is, the game's slowed down," Brown said.

The Longhorns never trailed against Baylor. But their opening drive, which saw Young complete just one of five passes, might have portended a sluggish afternoon against a weaker team when, as the season nears its end, an indifferent victory can mean lost points in the BCS ratings.

ABOVE: According to his teammates, there's no stopping Vince Young on the field. *Matt Rourke/American-Statesman*

Young recovered. On the next series, he found Limas Sweed for 45 yards to set up Texas' first touchdown.

"Vince again showed his maturity," said Texas offensive coordinator Greg Davis.

Nothing slowed the Longhorns for the rest of the day. When Young left the game, they were up by 55.

He expected that. For another game in this 9-0 season, Young got exactly what he expected.

"It's one of those things that's uncoachable," said receiver Quan Cosby.

"He's like that every week," said tailback Jamaal Charles.

TAYLOR OFF TO FAST START

BY CEDRIC GOLDEN, AUSTIN AMERICAN-STATESMAN

NOVEMBER 6, 2005

A childhood friend visited Ramonce Taylor at the Longhorns' team hotel Friday night and made a bold request.

"Why don't you score four touchdowns?" he asked.

That was a tall order, but Taylor made good on the wish Saturday in Texas' 62-0 rout of Baylor. Taylor scored a career-high four touchdowns (three rushing and one receiving) and was an integral part of a 1-2 running punch along with freshman Jamaal Charles, who added 72 yards and two touchdowns on 13 carries.

Taylor grew up in Temple before moving to Belton—where he played high school ball—but he claims both Central Texas towns as home. With a number of family members and friends in the stands at Floyd Casey Stadium on Saturday, he received his best news of the day during pregame drills, when he was told he would start at running back for the first time.

Typically, Taylor plays wide receiver for the Longhorns.

"It was great to come back and have a lot of people supporting me," said Taylor, who practiced primarily at running back this week. "I remember the last time I was in Waco, I had a bad game in high school, so I wanted to play well."

Taylor added three receptions for 43 yards, including a 42-yard touchdown reception. That play got him into a little trouble with Texas coach Mack Brown after Taylor unnecessarily dived into the end zone, drawing a 15-yard penalty for excessive celebration. Brown ordered Taylor to apologize to his teammates on the sideline.

"I guess I got a little too excited," Taylor said.

Taylor also accounted for 148 yards of offense while averaging 8.2 yards per touch. UT offensive coordinator Greg Davis said the plan was to have Taylor and Charles split the workload at running back, and run freshman Henry Melton in short-yardage situations. Junior Selvin Young is still not healthy after re-aggravating an ankle injury.

"R.T. brings so much speed to the game," Davis said. "He has the type of ball skills that give us a lot of options when he's in there."

Taylor made the most of his opportunity and showed an ability to carry the rushing load if Charles—who said he was 90 percent healthy for Saturday's game—has a setback with an ankle injury that's bothered him the past month.

"It was beautiful to see Ramonce running like that in front of his folks," Charles said. "I thought it was good for him to get a chance to do his thing."

ABOVE: Ramonce Taylor has proven his worth as both receiver and running back this season.

Ralph Barrera/American-Statesman

ROUTE 66

BY SUZANNE HALLIBURTON
AUSTIN AMERICAN-STATESMAN

Whether the trash talk was real or imagined, the Texas offense shared a perception Saturday afternoon that Kansas didn't hold them in such high esteem.

The Longhorns believed that the Jayhawks, who had been the best defense against the rush in the country, assumed that they would have an easy time mashing the Texas runners. In the Longhorns' eyes, there was too much back-patting coming out of Lawrence this week.

By game's end, in a 66-14 Big 12 Conference whitewash of a victory, the No. 2 Longhorns pointed to a powerful stat that was indicative of the one-sided nature of the contest.

Of Texas' 617 total yards, 336 came on the ground. Kansas had been limiting opponents to 64 yards—three Longhorns runners individually eclipsed that average and a fourth came within seven yards.

Whether it was starting tailback Ramonce Taylor or freshman flash Jamaal Charles or gutty walk-on Antwaun Hobbs, the Jayhawks had no

RIGHT: A UT fan predicts the future during the Longhorns' easy win over the Jayhawks. *Ralph Barrera/American-Statesman*

answer as eight Texas runners combined to average 6.3 yards a carry. And they accomplished this on an afternoon when quarterback Vince Young didn't try to turn the game with his dazzling running ability.

Instead, Young wounded the Jayhawks' defense with his arm, throwing for 281 yards and four touchdowns as he became the school's total all-time offensive leader.

"It makes your chest stick out," said Texas offensive tackle Jonathan Scott. "I'm so proud of this offense."

The Longhorns, as a team, proudly stuck out their chests at the end OF the game—Texas' last of the season at Royal-Memorial Stadium. Fans chanted "Rose Bowl, Rose Bowl," as the players ran off the field and into the locker room.

But before they can set their sights on the national championship game, they must defeat Texas A&M on Nov. 25 and then win the Big 12 Conference title game on Dec. 3. The victory—the Longhorns' 10th of the season—clinched the South Division for Texas.

Kansas coach Mark Mangino, whose team fell to 5-5, gushed over the Longhorns. "I don't think I've ever been on the field with a football team with so many big, strong, fast, talented kids," Mangino said.

Every aspect of the Texas team turned in significant plays, which made the game so lopsided.

The offense provided eight touchdowns and a field goal. Until Kansas running back Jon Cornish scampered around left end for a 59-yard touchdown with 14:14 to go in the third quarter, Texas had

OPPOSITE PAGE: Ramonce Taylor (11) congratulates Selvin Young (22) following Young's touchdown run in the fourth quarter. *Ralph Barrera/American-Statesman*

BELOW: Texas' Selvin Young (22) gained 57 yards on the ground against the Jayhawks. *Matt Rourke/American-Statesman*

scored 152 unanswered points, dating to the second quarter of the Oklahoma State game Oct. 29.

Special teams provided Aaron Ross' 71-yard punt return for a touchdown. It was his second touchdown of the year. Robert Killebrew's fumble recovery of a muffed kickoff, meanwhile, set up the Longhorns' second TD.

And playing cornerback, Ross picked off Kansas' Jason Swanson, returning the interception 31 yards to the KU 3. On the next play, Young threw his fourth touchdown pass to rarely used tight end Peter Ullman.

The defense was so overwhelming that Kansas didn't notch its initial first down until 10:13 to go before halftime. By then, the Longhorns owned a 42-0 lead. The Jayhawks gained 267 yards, but 224 came in the second half. By then, most of the Texas' first-teamers were sipping water on the sidelines. Young and the first-team offense played only one series in the second half.

The 66 points represented the second-most the Longhorns ever have scored in a decade of Big 12 play. And the 52 Texas put up by intermission tied the most scored in a half in school history.

In fact, the only time the game was competitive was when the Longhorns offense was lulling Kansas into a trap. On the opening two series, Texas offensive coordinator Greg Davis signaled for Young to pass on the first six plays. With temperatures nearing 80 degrees, Texas wanted the Jayhawks to expend energy rushing Young.

And they knew that Kansas was devoting much of its defense to thwarting the run, making the pass a better option. On those opening two series, Texas failed to make a first down.

Then, from the third series on, the Longhorns were nearly unstoppable.

"We wanted to show them that we were going to throw the ball all over the place to win the game," said Texas coach Mack Brown. "We weren't going to be stubborn (with the run)."

The long passes—Young had touchdown completions of 64 yards to Quan Cosby, 45 to Limas

Sweed and 29 to David Thomas—set up the Longhorns' outside running game, with option pitches and zone reads And when Kansas loosened its defense in order to tighten the corners, Texas abused the middle.

"They disrespected us, and we took that to heart," said Taylor, the team's leading rusher with 96 yards and two touchdowns. "We felt like we wanted to send a message and prove a point that it's not good to talk trash, to disrespect us and put us down like that."

	1st	2nd	3rd	4th	Final
Kansas	0	0	14	0	14
Texas	28	24	7	7	66

Scoring Summary

1st—**Texas** Sweed 4-yard pass from V. Young (Pino kick)—Three plays, 65 yards in 0:42.

Texas Charles 10-yard run (Pino kick)—1 play, 10 yards in 0:13.

Texas Cosby 64-yard pass from V. Young (Pino kick)—3 plays, 81 yards in 1:06.

Texas Ross 71-yard punt return (Pino kick).

2nd—**Texas** Taylor 8-yard run (Pino kick)—9 plays, 87 yards in 3:29.

Texas Thomas 29-yard pass from V. Young (Pino kick)—3 plays, 47 yards in 0:45.

Texas Ullman 3-yard pass from V. Young (Pino kick)—1 play, 3 yards in 0:06.

Texas Pino 35-yard field goal—9 plays, 54 yards in 1:44.

3rd—**Kansas** Cornish 59-yard run (Webb kick)—2 plays, 65 yards in 0:46.

Texas Taylor 12-yard run (Pino kick)—15 plays, 80 yards in 7:33.

Kansas McAnderson 15-yard run (Webb kick)—2 plays, 28 yards in 0:14.

4th—**Texas** S. Young 2-yard run (Phillips kick)—8 plays, 78 yards in 3:41.

Team Statistics

Category	KU	UT
First downs	9	29
Rushes-yards (Net)	22-119	53-336
Passing-yards (Net)	148	281
Passes Att-Comp-Int	35-17-1	28-19-1
Total offense plays-Yards	57-267	81-617
Fumble returns-Yards	0-0	0-0
Punt returns-Yards	2-10	4-91
Kickoff returns-Yards	7-116	1-21
Interception returns-Yards	1-18	1-31
Punts (Number-Avg)	11-42.6	5-35.4
Fumbles-lost	1-1	3-0
Sacks by (Number-Yards)	1-12	2-1
Penalties-yards	8-55	6-35
Possession time	25:34	34:26

OPPOSITE PAGE: Texas' David Thomas (16) hauls in this first-down catch in the first quarter over Kansas' Jerome Kemp.

Ralph Barrera/American-Statesman

NEVER A DOUBT

BY SUZANNE HALLIBURTON
AUSTIN AMERICAN-STATESMAN

It was third-and-2, with only a national championship on the line.

The Texas defenders, their goal line directly behind them, assumed that Texas A&M would run the ball—that surprise starter Stephen McGee would take the option around right end from the 10 or hand off to burly tailback Jorvorskie Lane, who had been abusing the middle of the Longhorns' line.

The Longhorns didn't know that they'd eventually prevail 40-29 to finish the regular season undefeated. What was apparent with 10 minutes to play was that the Aggies, the 26-point underdogs, were within a touchdown and a two-point conversion of tying the Longhorns.

At the snap, All-America tackle Rod Wright spun away from A&M guard Dominque Steamer and sacked McGee, who then fumbled away A&M's dreams of the greatest upset in Longhorns history.

"We never doubted we'd win," Wright said. "We're happy. We know we still have a lot of work to do. It's just how it is. We never get too excited, but we're happy."

All that stands now between Texas and the Rose Bowl is next Saturday's Big 12 championship game against Colorado or Iowa State.

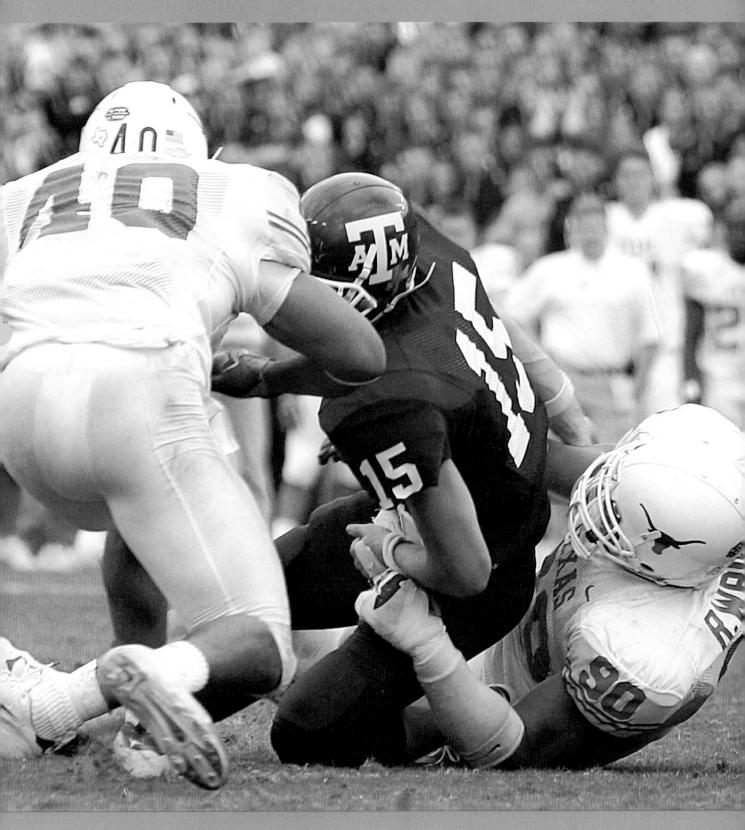

ABOVE: Texas' Robert Killebrew (40) and Rodrique Wright (90) bring down Texas A&M quarterback Stephen McGee to force a fumble during the fourth quarter. *Deborah Cannon/American-Statesman*

ABOVE: **Cedric Griffin returns a blocked punt for a touchdown in the third quarter.** *Deborah Cannon/American-Statesman*

OPPOSITE PAGE: **Texas' Rashad Bobino (44), Brian Orakpo (98) and Frank Okam (97) bring down Texas A&M quarterback Stephen McGee.**
Deborah Cannon/American-Statesman

The Longhorns posted their 11th victory—the first undefeated regular season in 22 years—and allowed themselves a bit of an excessive celebration on the sideline. Matt Nordgren and William Winston were among the players who dumped a cooler of icy water on coach Mack Brown before they gathered en masse at the southeast corner of Kyle Field to celebrate with their fans.

"Give our football team credit for not panicking," Brown said. "We did the things we needed to do to win. It's so hard to go 11-0 anymore. You're playing against a national championship-like effort every weekend because the other team wants to beat you so bad."

The annual rivalry, which dates to 1894, typically is tightly contested. The Aggies' motivation had everything to do with playing one more game—a victory would have given them the required six wins for a bowl invitation. Instead, they ended the year 5-6, the Aggies' second losing season in three years.

"It's a dangerous team out there—one that has nothing to lose," Wright said.

Said A&M coach Dennis Franchione, "We probably just made a few too many miscues there to be able to beat a No. 1- or No. 2-ranked team in the nation."

ABOVE: Texas defenders Larry Dibbles (92), Rodderick Muckelroy (38) and Michael Griffin (27) tackle A&M quarterback Stephen McGee.

Jay Janner/American-Statesman

The A&M defense made few mistakes when taking on the Longhorns, holding them 165 yards below their average.

Texas quarterback Vince Young suffered through his worst performance of the year. Although he faced the worst pass defense in the country, he completed only 13 of his 24 passes for 162 yards, with a touchdown pass to fullback Ahmard Hall.

Young also couldn't run the ball effectively, rushing 11 times for 19 yards. He was sacked three times, as the Longhorns' offensive line struggled to block the Aggies' interior linemen.

He was intercepted once and his fumble early in the third quarter set up a McGee touchdown, giving the Aggies a 22-21 lead.

"They gave us all they had," Young said of A&M. "All that matters to me is that we won."

The Longhorns' most effective rusher was Ramonce Taylor, who gained 102 yards, 71 of them in the second half, scoring two touchdowns. A&M's tackles often were in the backfield, making it impossible for the Longhorns to effectively use the zone read, their base running play.

The Texas defense struggled mightily against A&M's offense because McGee nearly beat Texas with his feet, rushing for two touchdowns and 108 yards on 24 carries.

McGee had found out Tuesday he would make his first career start, after Aggie coaches realized that Reggie McNeal's sprained left ankle still was too tender to play. However, Franchione didn't announce his decision publicly. Texas prepared for both quarterbacks, but the first clue the Longhorns had that McNeal wouldn't play is when the senior showed up for pregame warmups in blue jeans.

A&M used much more of the blue-collar option than Texas expected. McGee found most of his success running to the outside, which loosened up the middle for the 265-pound Lane, who battered the Longhorns for 104 yards on 17 carries. Lane's 35-yard touchdown pass to Jason Carter also proved to be the longest throw of the game.

With both sides of the ball struggling, the Longhorns' special-teams play was critical in the second half. Rashad Bobino, who was an upback on the punt team, took the snap and converted a fourth-and-1 midway through the third quarter, setting up Taylor's eventual 8-yard touchdown run. That gave Texas a 28-22 lead.

	1st	2nd	3rd	4th	Final
Texas	14	7	13	6	40
Texas A&M	9	6	14	0	29

Scoring Summary

1st— **Texas** Melton 8-yard run (Pino kick)—3 plays, 17 yards in 0:19.

Texas Taylor 5-yard run (Pino kick)—7 plays, 48 yards in 1:56.

A&M Pegram 31-yard field goal—12 plays, 67 yards in 3:57.

A&M Carter 35-yard pass from Lane (Pegram pass intercepted)—1 play, 35 yards in 0:07.

2nd— **A&M** Leone 16-yard run (Lane rush fumbled)—7 plays, 85 yards in 3:51.

Texas Hall 14-yard pass from V. Young (Pino kick)—7 plays, 77 yards in 2:44.

3rd— **A&M** McGee 11-yard run (Pegram kick)—2 plays, 15 yards in 0:53.

Texas Taylor 8-yard run (Pino kick)—10 plays, 80 yards in 4:21.

Texas Griffin 11-yard blocked punt return (Pino kick failed).

A&M McGee 1-yard run (Pegram kick)—8 plays, 65 yards in 3:36.

4th— **Texas** Pino 41-yard field goal, 6-56 2:14.

Texas Pino 29-yard field goal, 6-20 3:19.

Team Statistics

Category	Texas	Texas A & M
First Downs	18	22
Rushes-Yards (Net)	42-174	52-277
Passing-Yards (Net)	162	118
Passes Att-Comp-Int	24-13-1	24-10-1
Total Offense Plays-Yards	66-336	76-395
Fumble Returns-Yards	0-0	0-0
Punt Returns-Yards	2-25	1-0
Kickoff Returns-Yards	1-21	6-117
Interception Returns-Yards	1-2	1-17
Punts (Number-Avg)	3-33.7	5-27.2
Fumbles-Lost	4-2	4-2
Sacks By (Number-Yards)	4-45	3-32
Penalties-Yards	3-15	9-77
Possession Time	24:43	35:17

A drive later, Michael Griffin blocked an A&M punt, which was picked up by Cedric Griffin and returned 11 yards for a touchdown. That gave Texas a 34-22 lead with 5:45 remaining in the third quarter. A fumble recovery by Ryan Palmer off a muffed Aggies punt also allowed Texas to whittle time off the clock.

But the Texas defense finally came up with the key plays to take the Aggies out of the game.

There was Wright's forced fumble, on the 11th play of what had been a 71-yard drive. Then, on A&M's final chance to get back in the game, safety Michael Huff blitzed McGee and sacked him for a 19-yard loss. Huff stepped to strongside linebacker on the play, after realizing that the Longhorns had the wrong personnel package on the field.

"It was a one-touchdown (type) game, and we had to have someone step up and make a play," said Texas co-defensive coordinator Gene Chizik. "Obviously, we did. Your character always comes out in rivalry games."

ABOVE: **Coach Mack Brown gets doused with the contents of the water cooler following the Longhorns win.**
Jay Janner/American-Statesman

OPPOSITE PAGE: **Henry Melton celebrates his first-quarter touchdown run.** *Deborah Cannon/American-Statesman*

Big 12 Championship
December 3, 2005
Reliant Stadium
Houston, Texas

EASY DOZEN

BY SUZANNE HALLIBURTON
AUSTIN AMERICAN-STATESMAN

By game's end, a Big 12 championship in hand and a national championship in sight, the Longhorns' "flow session" was in full groove.

Normally, it's a private, players-only affair conducted during Saturday bus rides to the stadium. This time, it was postgame and public, as dozens of Longhorns clustered near their sideline, chanting and bobbing in unison, waving red and yellow roses.

Quarterback Vince Young was swinging his shoulders and dipping his hips in a free-flowing victory dance. Defensive tackle Larry Dibbles was in the middle of the group, leading the chants.

"We're going . . . going. Back . . . back. To Cali . . . Cali."

Saturday's 70-3 victory—the most lopsided championship in Big 12 history—more than qualified Texas for the national title game against top-ranked Southern California at the Rose Bowl on Jan. 4.

Official invitations will be issued this afternoon, but there was no way human voters or the rankings of six computers could deny Texas one of the two championship spots.

The players, who have been so disciplined and focused since the summer's voluntary workouts,

ABOVE: **Texas players hoist the Big 12 Championship trophy.** *Ralph Barrera/American-Statesman*

finally let loose on the field moments after their 12th victory of the season and 19th in a row.

"It's good, sometimes, to stop and smell the roses," Dibbles gushed. "We're doing what feels good."

Moments before the game ended, coach Mack Brown was doused with a bucket of ice and Gatorade. He just laughed and tried to fix his hair for the postgame network interviews.

"I'm so proud," Brown said. "This bunch has been fighting the pressure of going back to the Rose Bowl since the Oklahoma game. It's been the most amazing thing I've ever seen.

"I didn't think we handled it as well last week (against Texas A&M). But the guys were able to focus on their goal at hand today."

The outcome was decided early—perhaps when Brian Robison blocked a 31-yard field-goal attempt by Buffaloes All-America kicker Mason Crosby to protect Texas' 14-0 lead with 1:45 remaining in the first quarter.

By halftime, the margin was 42-3. Young and the Longhorns offensive starters left the game with 10 minutes to go in the third quarter, with the score 63-3.

Reserve quarterback Matt Nordgren then led the Longhorns on their final scoring drive that culminated in Henry Melton's 1-yard plunge with 7:36 to go in the quarter.

It was the eighth most lopsided victory in Texas' 113-year history.

So why were the Longhorns so dominant?

ABOVE: Henry Melton (37) scores a first-quarter touchdown against Colorado. *Jay Janner/American-Statesman*

Colorado, which boasted the second-best rushing defense in the country, could not control the Longhorns' offense.

Texas stayed in a hurry-up, no-huddle scheme through the first half, evenly mixing up runs and passes. The intent was to stretch the Colorado defense and widen the Longhorns' running lanes. It was 100 percent effective as Texas averaged 7.2 yards a snap in the first half.

In his two quarters of play, Young completed 14 of 17 passes for 193 yards and three touchdowns.

He and Limas Sweed combined on two impressive plays. One was a 31-yarder on a post route that gave Texas a 28-3 lead with 11:23 remaining in the first half. Later in the quarter, Young and Sweed combined on a crossing route for a 38-yard gain that set up the quarterback's touchdown toss to tight end David Thomas.

On the ground, Young gained 58 yards on eight carries, while Jamaal Charles provided 62 yards and two touchdowns. Melton also scored two touchdowns, while Selvin Young came off the bench for a 4-yard score.

"You saw it—we had everybody covered and (Young) takes off for 10 yards and scores," Colorado coach Gary Barnett said. "You don't have an answer or solution for it, or we sure didn't."

Defensively, Texas withstood some early tinkering by Colorado. The Buffaloes threw in some option plays, noting that the Longhorns had problems with it against Texas A&M eight days ago. They also used new formations to better feature their big tight ends, often lining up Joel Klopfenstein and Quinn Sypniewski on the same side with a wide receiver.

Colorado had early success, but turnovers proved critical. On their opening drive, the Buffaloes drove to the Texas 36, before safety Michael Huff stripped Hugh Charles of the ball, allowing Robison to recover the fumble.

The Buffaloes then suffered two more fumbles and an interception. In addition, they had a field-goal attempt blocked by Robison. And early in the third quarter, Colorado's punt protection team forgot about Michael Griffin, who burst through the middle of the line for an uncontested swat. Brandon Foster fell on the ball in the end zone for the touchdown.

The Longhorns, knowing they had the game won, grew antsy as the fourth quarter slowly unfolded, as Nordgren, and then walk-on quarterback Matt McCoy handed off the ball on most every play to keep from running up the score.

With about two minutes to go, fans began passing roses to the players. The postgame celebration then lasted for more than 30 minutes on the field of Reliant Stadium, as Brown accepted the Longhorns' first football championship trophy in nine years and then a bouquet from the Rose Bowl representative.

Players shed their shoulder pads and put on new burnt-orange T-shirts and white caps proclaiming them Big 12 champions. Some did victory laps, as they clutched roses in their teeth. Griffin hopped into the south end zone stands and took photographs with the fans.

OPPOSITE PAGE: Vince Young lifts the Big 12 Championship trophy over his head while coach Mack Brown salutes the crowd.
Deborah Cannon/American-Statesman

In his postgame comments, Vince Young recalled the energy-sapping summer drills and all the work the Longhorns put in since beating Michigan in last year's Rose Bowl.

"Every time, we'd break (the huddle)," Young recalled, "we'd say, 'Big 12.'"

One goal was accomplished Saturday afternoon, with a more significant one looming two time zones and a month away.

Huff was asked whether Texas—the first Longhorns group in history to post 12 victories in a season—is the best team in the country. He didn't pause before answering.

"I feel we are," he said.

	1st	2nd	3rd	4th	Final
Texas	14	28	28	0	70
Colorado	0	3	0	0	3

Scoring Summary

1st— **Texas** Melton 1-yard run (Pino kick)—7-65 1:56.
Texas Charles 3-yard pass from V. Young (Pino kick)—8-52 3:19.
2nd— **Colorado** Crosby 25-yard field goal—4 plays, 3 yards in 0:19.
Texas V. Young 2-yard run (Pino kick)—7 plays, 46 yards in 2:48.
Texas Sweed 31-yard pass from V. Young (Pino kick)—1 play, 31 yards in 0:07.
Texas Thomas 8-yard pass from V. Young (Pino kick)—4 plays, 44 yards in 1:44.
Texas Charles 2-yard run (Pino kick)—9 plays, 71 yards in 2:44.
3rd— **Texas** S. Young 4-yard run (Pino kick)—8 plays, 68 yards in 3:34.
Texas Foster 0-yard blocked punt return (Pino kick).
Texas Charles 26-yard run (Pino kick)—1 play, 26 yards in 0:08.
Texas Melton 1-yard run (Pino kick)—6 plays, 16 yards in 2:18.

Team Statistics

Category	Texas	Colorado
First downs	26	12
Rushes-Yards (Net)	57-268	26-82
Passing-Yards (Net)	218	109
Passes Att-Comp-Int	19-16-1	32-15-1
Total offense plays-Yards	76-486	58-191
Fumble Returns-Yards	0-0	0-0
Punt Returns-Yards	4-42	1-3
Kickoff Returns-Yards	2-83	5-96
Interception Returns-Yards	1-11	1-21
Punts (Number-Avg)	2-34.0	7-32.6
Fumbles-Lost	0-0	4-3
Sacks By (Number-Yards)	0-0	0-0
Penalties-Yards	11-93	8-74
Possession Time	36:06	23:54

TITLE HOPES BLOOM

BY SUZANNE HALLIBURTON, AUSTIN AMERICAN-STATESMAN

DECEMBER 5, 2005

L et the national championship buildup begin. On Sunday, the University of Texas football team officially received one of two coveted spots in the Bowl Championship Series national title game to be played at the Rose Bowl on Jan. 4 in Pasadena, Calif. The undefeated Longhorns will meet two-time defending national champion Southern California on college football's biggest stage.

The buildup for the game had started even before Texas won the Big 12 championship Saturday and USC completed its second straight unbeaten season. The hype will reach a crescendo over the next 30 days with talk of whether the Longhorns, who have the highest-scoring offense in the country, can end the Trojans' 34-game victory streak.

"We couldn't ask for a better game," said Rose Bowl President Libby Evans Wright, who scouted the Longhorns in person Nov. 25 when they played Texas A&M. "The theme of the Rose Bowl this year is 'It's magical.' And we believe this game is magical."

It certainly is a favorite of ABC television, considering the Trojans and Longhorns, statistically, are the two top offenses in the country.

The game will match the glitz of USC and its star-powered duo of quarterback Matt Leinart and tailback Reggie Bush against Texas' dynamic quarterback Vince Young and a dominant defense.

"If this isn't fun, then you need to find something else to do," said Texas coach Mack Brown, who was in New York on Sunday to accept the invitation on ABC's bowl selection show.

Southern Cal finished the season as the No. 1 team in the final BCS standings released Sunday, based on the USA Today coaches poll, the Harris Interactive poll of former administrators and coaches, and the average of six computer rankings. Texas, ranked second by the human polls and first by the computer average, was No. 2 overall.

This is the first time since the BCS' inception in 1998 that the top two teams in the initial rankings in October made it unscathed to the championship game.

In the three other BCS bowls, Penn State and Florida State will meet in the Orange Bowl, Ohio State will play Notre Dame in the Fiesta Bowl, and West Virginia will face Georgia in the Sugar Bowl.

Texas will receive $1.48 million to cover its Rose Bowl expenses. It will share its remaining $14.5 million Rose Bowl payout with the other 11 members of the Big 12 Conference.

The team will leave Austin on Dec. 28 and stay in Beverly Hills, Calif., for eight days, with Longhorn and Trojan players participating in news conferences for the entire stretch.

Brown will stay in New York until Thursday to attend festivities for the National Football Foundation Hall of Fame induction. Longhorn

ABOVE: Vince Young holds a rose in his mouth in celebration of Texas' Rose Bowl bid. *Jay Janner/American-Statesman*

BEYOND Xs AND Os

"If this isn't fun, then you need to find something else to do."

–Texas head coach Mack Brown

great Roosevelt Leaks is among those being inducted into college football's hall of fame on Tuesday.

Back in Austin, there was no official team function Sunday to watch as the invitations were unveiled. But the team did meet Sunday night to talk about the Rose Bowl and the logistics of getting there. This morning, coaches will begin formulating a game plan by studying tapes of the Trojans' 12 victories this fall.

Rod Wright, the Longhorns' All-America defensive tackle, said Texas plans on dominating, rather than trying to stay close to the Trojans, a team trying to win a historic third straight championship.

"If you prepare like that, then it can happen," Wright said. "We're not going to be overwhelmed."

For Texas, it will be a return trip to Pasadena. The Longhorns, after finishing the 2004 regular season 10-1, earned a BCS at-large berth to the Rose Bowl. On Jan. 1, they beat Michigan.

USC won the Rose Bowl after the 2003 season.

Coach Pete Carroll acknowledged that his Trojans could feel the pressure if they allow themselves to be distracted.

"You'd be surprised how little emphasis is put on our winning streak," Carroll said. "It doesn't serve you to talk about what's happened in the past. The amount of pressure is there if you allow it to affect you."

If Texas has its way, the hype will be part of the spectacle. The Longhorns want it to be fun and not a burden. It definitely will be a new experience. Texas last played for a national title in 1983. It hasn't won one since 1970.

Greg Davis, the Longhorns' offensive coordinator, said several coaches of other teams called him during the season's stretch run.

They all had one common description of the way the Longhorns were playing.

"They told me it looked like our kids were having a lot of fun," Davis said. "Our kids are going to enjoy the big stage."

ABOVE: Cedric Griffin leads his teammates around the stadium to slap hands with UT fans following Texas' defeat of Colorado to clinch the Big 12 Championship. *Ralph Barrera/American-Statesman*

Vince Young is showered with confetti after the Longhorns' Rose Bowl victory.

Rodolfo Gonzalez/American-Statesman

Rose Bowl: National Championship
January 4, 2006
Pasadena, California

FOREVER YOUNG!

BY SUZANNE HALLIBURTON
AUSTIN AMERICAN-STATESMAN

I t was fourth-and-5 from Southern California's 8-yard line. The clock was stopped at 26 seconds. Texas was down by five points, and all that was on the line was the Longhorns' first national championship in 35 years and the chance to pull out a victory on possibly the biggest stage in college football history.

No one said a word in the huddle as Vince Young called the play.

Split end Limas Sweed was to run a streak down the sideline into the end zone. Tight end David Thomas was to go to the opposite corner of the end zone and hope that Young could lob the ball to him over the safety. Quan Cosby, lined up in the slot, was ordered to run a slant and dash past the coverage to be Young's third outlet, to at least pick up the yards needed for a first down and another chance.

When the ball was snapped, however, USC had everyone covered. So Young—as he did on 18 previous carries—tucked the ball away and sprinted into the end zone, sucking the air from thousands of the hometown Trojan fans who were desperately hoping some USC defender might pull off the miracle play.

ABOVE: **Vince Young races across the goal line for the game-winning touchdown in Texas' 41-38 victory over USC.**
Rodolfo Gonzalez/American-Statesman

113

ABOVE: Texas' Michael Griffin intercepts a pass in the end zone over USC's Steve Smith during the second quarter.

Rodolfo Gonzalez/American-Statesman

It seemed so appropriate that Young had saved the most spectacular performance of his football career for the Rose Bowl, its 93,986 fans and millions in a national television audience. With his third touchdown of the game, the remnants of what had been a 12-point USC lead disappeared for good.

Southern California, with its two Heisman Trophy winners and possibly college football's best all-time offense, was favored to extend its winning streak to 35 games and claim its third straight national championship, something no team had ever accomplished.

Instead, it was Texas that strutted out of the Rose Bowl with the crystal national championship trophy and a winning streak at 20 games.

Thirteen of those games came in this perfect season. And the victory gave the proud Texas program not only its fourth national title, but also its 800th all-time win.

Young felt that the Longhorns were not getting their due in the four weeks leading up to the game. And he played as if he had something to prove.

"We didn't get no respect. But nobody gave us 12-0," said Young, as he held court with the national media after the game.

Young, as he's done so many times before in Texas' most critical games, directed the Longhorns on a fourth-quarter comeback to claim the national

BELOW: Vince Young (center) celebrates a national championship with teammates after Texas' 41-38 victory in the Rose Bowl.
Ralph Barrera/American-Statesman

"That's the best single-game performance I've ever had against me."

–USC coach Pete Carroll, speaking about Vince Young

	1st	2nd	3rd	4th	Final
Texas	0	16	7	18	41
USC	7	3	14	14	38

Scoring Summary
1st– **USC** White 4-yard run (Danelo kick)–5 plays, 46 yards.
2nd– **Texas** Pino 46-yard field goal–9 plays, 52 yards.
　　Texas S. Young 12-yard run (Pino kick failed)–7 plays, 80 yards.
　　Texas Taylor 30-yard run (Pino kick)–4 plays, 51 yards.
　　USC Danelo 43-yard field goal–11 plays, 54 yards.
3rd– **USC** White 3-yard run (Danelo kick)–7 plays, 62 yards.
　　Texas V. Young 14-yard run (Pino kick)–7 plays, 80 yards.
　　USC White 12-yard run (Danelo kick)–9 plays, 74 yards.
4th– **USC** Bush 26-yard run (Danelo kick)–9 plays, 80 yards.
　　Texas Pino 34-yard field goal–9 plays, 52 yards.
　　USC Jarrett 22-yard pass from Leinart (Danelo kick)–4 plays, 80 yards.
　　Texas V. Young 17-yard run (Pino kick)–8 plays, 69 yards.
　　Texas V. Young 8-yard run (V. Young 2 point conversion)–10 plays, 56 yards.

Team Statistics
Category	USC	Texas
First Downs	30	30
Rushes-Yards (net)	41-209	36-289
Passing Yards (net)	365	267
Passes Att-Comp-Int	41-29-1	40-30-0
Total Offense Plays-Yards	82-574	76-556
Punt Returns-Yards	0-0	2-19
Kickoff Returns-Yards	7-130	1-29
Interception Returns-Yards	0-0	1-0
Punts (Number-Avg)	2-41.5	2-34
Fumbles-Lost	1-1	4-1
Sacks By (Number-Yards)	0-0	3-15
Penalties-Yards	5-30	4-34
Possession Time	32:00	28:00

championship. He rushed for 200 yards and three touchdowns. He completed 30 of 40 passes for 267 yards. The Texas offensive line did not allow a sack.

"That's the best single-game performance I've ever had against me," said USC coach Pete Carroll.

With 6:42 left in the game, USC appeared to lock up the victory when quarterback Matt Leinart threw a 22-yard dart to Dwayne Jarrett for the touchdown that gave the Trojans a 38-26 lead.

Young responded by leading Texas on an 8-play, 69-yard drive to pull Texas within five at 38-33. The drive took 2 minutes and 4 seconds, pumped hope into the Longhorn faithful and returned to the defense the seemingly impossible task of stopping the Trojans.

At that point in the game, the odds were with USC. The Trojans had amassed 547 offensive yards. Leinart had missed only 10 of his 38 passes. LenDale White had amassed 123 yards.

And yet, on a fourth-down play that would have denied Young his final heroics, Longhorn defensive end Brian Robison, tackle Larry Dibbles, cornerback Aaron Ross and safety Michael Huff hit White head on, stopping his powerful run less than the length of a hand from the first down.

With that, the defense confidently returned the controls to Young.

"We had Vince," Huff said. "Vince is great at this kind of thing."

Great, indeed. Ten plays later, Young put Texas back on top for good.

National championship shirts and hats appeared out of nowhere. Ecstatic players were mugging for every camera in sight. The celebration was expected to last late into the evening.

"We have the whole city," exclaimed tackle Frank Okam.

"I said we'd do it," said linebacker Rashad Bobino. "And we did it."

OPPOSITE PAGE: The Longhorns had plenty of star power to counter the celebrities hanging around USC. Here, actor Matthew McConaughey, who was featured prominently in ABC's pregame show, speaks with quarterback Vince Young.
Deborah Cannon/American-Statesman

Rose Bowl: National Championship
January 4, 2006
Pasadena, California

PERFECT FINISH FOR HORNS

BY KEVIN ROBBINS
AUSTIN AMERICAN-STATESMAN

The stampede ended with a late and legendary run, the kind of impossibly possible play that leaves a player branded forever.

Vince Young now bears that mark. It's the mark shared by the icons of Texas football, the mark that defines the players who took the team to glorious places.

With 30 seconds remaining Wednesday night and one chance left to win, Young cradled the ball and dashed deeper into the lore of Texas football. His thrilling 8-yard touchdown run in the presence of 93,986 spectators at the Rose Bowl sealed the national championship.

Texas beat two-time defending champion USC 41-38 in the waning moments of a title game that sparkled like the glitter shot from the cannons on the field when time ran out on the Trojans' hopes. Texas extended its winning streak to 20 games and ended USC's at 34.

The victory never was sure. The Trojans scored first after Texas fumbled a punt. The Longhorns replied with 16 points and carried a six-point lead into halftime.

ABOVE: Ramonce Taylor scores a touchdown in the second quarter on a 30-yard run to put Texas up 15-7. *Deborah Cannon/American-Statesman*

Then the Rose Bowl became the game that everyone had anticipated. A lively exhibition of immortal plays and epic offense emerged from the intermission, as if the teams realized in their dressing rooms that football is fun when the ball moves, the scoreboard spins and the partisan spectators cheer so rabidly they bend the trees in the San Gabriel Mountains.

The Trojans scored. The Longhorns scored. Then they did it all again until, as any great game must, a great player helped a great team win.

"The ball was all over the field," said USC head coach Pete Carroll.

USC's dangerous running backs, LenDale White and Heisman Trophy winner Reggie Bush, churned out more than 200 yards. They scored four touchdowns.

"That offense . . . we couldn't stop them. We could not get them off of the field," said Texas head coach Mack Brown.

But Texas never surrendered. Even down by more than a touchdown in the second half, the

BELOW: Four USC defenders attempt to tackle running back Selvin Young.

Jay Janner/American-Statesman

ABOVE: Kicker David Pino (15) celebrates with William Winston (78) during the first half after making a 46-yard field goal.
Jay Janner/American-Statesman

ABOVE: Texas defenders Brian Robison (39), Roy Miller (75) and Rodrique Wright bring down USC running back LenDale White in the fourth quarter. *Jay Janner/American-Statesman*

"I think he's one of the greatest players to ever play college football."

–Texas coach Mack Brown, speaking about Vince Young

Longhorns believed they were somehow destined to win.

"It was really surreal," said Brown said. "We never ever really thought we could lose the ballgame."

"I really ain't got no words for it right now," said Texas defensive tackle Larry Dibbles, who wandered the crowded field after the win.

Cheerleader Tyler Carr ran to the 50-yard line and planted a Texas flag in the ground. Assistant coach Mike Tolleson found Dibbles and embraced his sweaty and grass-stained uniform.

"I love you," the coach told his player.

Cornerback Cedric Griffin fell to the ground and stared at the sky.

"We won for our fans," he said. "We won for ourselves."

Defensive tackle Frank Okam remembered watching from the sidelines as the final drive evolved.

"I knew Vince was going to make a play," Okam said. "We'd come too far for it to end."

"I think he's one of the greatest players to ever play college football," Brown said of Young.

Months of anticipation ended as night came to Southern California and one of the most beloved stadiums in sports.

Texas swept its schedule to win 12 games, including the Big 12 Championship over Colorado, for the first time in history. The Longhorns claimed their first conference title on December 3, the same day USC beat UCLA to also go 12-0 to assure its place with Texas in the Rose Bowl.

Thousands of Longhorn fans immediately contacted travel agents.

There were so many orange hats on shirts in Beverly Hills this week that Rodeo Drive looked like the Drag—with a Mikimoto boutique instead of a Co-Op. On a cool Tuesday morning in Los Angeles, a twosome wore Texas windshirts at Rancho Park Golf Course.

Southern California—all tropical pastels and vibrant coastal tones—burned in a Western shade of orange.

Like the Rose Bowl did late Wednesday night, when legends were made again. When the Longhorns left the field, they left as the national champions of college football, the first Texas team to hold that coveted trophy since Darrell Royal's team of 1970.

"It's been a long time coming," offensive lineman Justin Blalock said.

TEAM STATS

Texas Team Statistics (as of January 5, 2006)

Category	Texas	Opp.
Scoring	652	213
Points Per Game	50.2	16.4
First Downs	321	224
Rushing	180	106
Passing	121	99
Penalty	20	19
Rushing Yardage	3,574	1,702
Yards Gained Rushing	3,866	2,115
Yards Lost Rushing	292	413
Rushing Attempts	605	461
Average Per Rush	5.9	3.7
Average Per Game	274.9	130.9
Touchdowns Rushing	55	15
Passing Yardage	3,083	2,236
Att-Comp-Int	336-218-11	436-223-11
Average Per Pass	9.2	5.1
Average Per Catch	14.1	10.0

Category	Texas	Opp.
Average Per Game	237.2	172.0
Touchdowns Passing	26	10
Total Offense	6,657	3,938
Total Plays	941	897
Average Per Play	7.1	4.4
Average Per Game	512.1	302.9
Kick Returns (Number-Yards)	22-593	80-1522
Punt Returns (Number-Yards)	43-671	10-70
Int Returns (Number-Yards)	11-90	11-151
Kick Return Average	27.0	19.0
Punt Return Average	15.6	7.0
Int Return Average	8.2	13.7
Fumbles-Lost	35-9	27-16
Penalties-Yards	99-852	106-845
Average Per Game	65.5	65.0
Punts-Yards	38-1444	89-3485
Average Per Punt	38.0	39.2

Category	Texas	Opp.
Net punt average	36.2	31.6
Time of Possession (Game)	30:54	29:06
Third-Down Conversions	86/173	61/200
Third-Down Percentage	50%	30%
Fourth-Down Conversions	12/20	10/21
Fourth-Down Percentage	60%	48%
Sacks By-Yards	34-268	14-102
Miscellaneous Yards	97	0
Touchdowns Scored	88	25
Field Goals-Attempts	14-18	14-20
PAT-Attempts	76-85	21-22
Attendance (Average)	83,333	68,446

Score By Quarters

Team	1st	2nd	3rd	4th	Total
Texas	160	218	158	116	652
Opponents	66	48	58	41	213

Individual Offensive Statistics

Rushing

Player	GP	Att	Gain	Loss	Net	Avg	TD	Long	Avg/G
Young, Vince	13	155	1,186	136	1,050	6.8	12	80	80.8
Charles, Jamaal	13	119	906	28	878	7.4	11	80	67.5
Taylor, Ramonce	13	76	561	48	513	6.8	12	57	39.5
Young, Selvin	11	96	487	26	461	4.8	8	28	41.9
Melton, Henry	13	87	434	2	432	5.0	10	27	33.2
Ogbonnaya, Chris	8	22	79	3	76	3.5	1	22	9.5
Nordgren, Matt	12	12	52	14	38	3.2	1	11	3.2
McCoy, Matt	4	6	39	8	31	5.2	0	25	7.8
Pittman, Billy	13	2	28	0	28	14.0	0	19	2.2
Houston, Michael	2	3	27	0	27	9.0	0	14	13.5
Hobbs, Antwaun	2	9	31	4	27	3.0	0	12	13.5
Ballew, Scott	2	4	14	0	14	3.5	0	9	7.0
Hall, Ahmard	13	1	10	0	10	10.0	0	10	0.8
Bobino, Rashad	13	1	6	0	6	6.0	0	6	0.5
Myers, Marcus	7	4	6	1	5	1.2	0	3	0.7
Team	13	8	0	22	-22	-2.8	0	0	-1.7
Total	13	605	3,866	292	3,574	5.9	55	80	274.9
Opponents	13	461	2,115	413	1,702	3.7	15	59	130.9

Passing

Player	GP	Effic	Att-Comp-Int	Pct	Yds	TD	Long	Avg/G
Young, Vince	13	163.95	325-212-10	65.2	3,036	26	75	233.5
Nordgren, Matt	12	72.25	11-6-1	54.5	47	0	22	3.9
Total	13	160.94	336-218-11	64.9	3,083	26	75	237.2
Opponents	13	96.75	436-223-11	51.1	2,236	10	49	72.0

Receiving

Player	GP	No	Yds	Avg	TD	Long	Avg/G
Thomas, David	13	50	613	12.3	5	32	47.2
Sweed, Limas	13	36	545	15.1	5	45	41.9
Pittman, Billy	13	34	750	22.1	5	75	57.7
Taylor, Ramonce	13	27	265	9.8	3	42	20.4
Carter, Brian	10	18	263	14.6	0	40	26.3
Cosby, Quan	13	15	270	18.0	2	64	20.8
Charles, Jamaal	13	14	157	11.2	2	36	12.1
Jones, Nate	13	9	67	7.4	1	14	5.2
Young, Selvin	11	5	21	4.2	0	14	1.9
Hall, Ahmard	13	3	42	14.01	0	5	3.2
Tweedie, Neale	13	2	49	24.5	1	28	3.8
Gatewood, Tyrell	13	2	13	6.5	0	9	1.0
Walker, George	5	1	22	22.0	0	22	4.4
Ullman, Peter	11	1	3	3.0	1	3	0.3
Ogbonnaya, Chris	8	1	3	3.0	0	3	0.4
Total	13	218	3,083	14.1	26	75	237.2
Opponents	13	223	2,236	10.0	10	49	172.0

Punt Returns

Player	No	Yds	Avg	TD	Long
Ross, Aaron	34	500	14.7	2	88
Cosby, Quan	6	92	15.3	0	38
Griffin, Michael	3	68	22.7	0	0
Foster, Brandon	0	0	0.0	1	0
Griffin, Cedric	0	11	0.0	1	11
Total	43	671	15.6	4	88
Opponents	10	70	7.0	0	32

Interceptions

Player	No	Yds	Avg	TD	Long
Griffin, Michael	3	0	0.0	0	0
Ross, Aaron	3	40	13.3	0	31
Harris, Aaron	1	30	30.0	0	30
Huff, Michael	1	11	11.0	0	11
Kelson, Drew	1	-2	-2.0	0	0
Crowder, Tim	1	0	0.0	0	0
Brown, Tarell	1	11	11.0	0	11
Total	11	90	8.2	0	31
Opponents	11	151	13.7	0	37

Kick Returns

Player	No	Yds	Avg	TD	Long
Taylor, Ramonce	15	441	29.4	0	54
Brown, Tarell	5	108	21.6	0	34
Cosby, Quan	1	30	30.0	0	30
Hall, Ahmard	1	14	14.0	0	14
Total	22	593	27.0	0	54
Opponents	80	1,522	19.0	0	47

Fumble Returns

Player	No	Yds	Avg	TD	Long
Wright, Rodrique	1	67	67.0	1	67
Huff, Michael	1	21	21.0	1	21
Robison, Brian	1	9	9.0	0	9
Okam, Frank	0	0	0.0	1	0
Total	3	97	32.3	3	67
Opponents	0	0	0.0	0	0

Scoring

Player	TD	FGs	Kick	Rush	Rcv	Pass	DXP	Saf	Points
Pino, David	0	14-18	71-77	0-0	0	0-0	0	0	113
Taylor, Ramonce	15	0-0	0-0	0-0	0	0-0	0	0	90
Charles, Jamaal	13	0-0	0-0	0-0	0	0-0	0	0	78
Young, Vince	12	0-0	0-0	1-1	0	1-2	0	0	74
Melton, Henry	10	0-0	0-0	0-0	0	0-0	0	0	60
Young, Selvin	8	0-0	0-0	0-0	0	0-0	0	0	48
Thomas, David	5	0-0	0-0	0-0	0	0-0	0	0	30
Pittman, Billy	5	0-0	0-0	0-0	0	0-0	0	0	30
Sweed, Limas	5	0-0	0-0	0-0	0	0-0	0	0	30
Ross, Aaron	2	0-0	0-0	0-0	0	0-0	0	0	12
Cosby, Quan	2	0-0	0-0	0-0	0	0-0	0	0	12
Hall, Ahmard	1	0-0	0-0	0-0	1	0-0	0	0	8
Okam, Frank	1	0-0	0-0	0-0	0	0-0	0	0	6
Foster, Brandon	1	0-0	0-0	0-0	0	0-0	0	0	6
Griffin, Cedric	1	0-0	0-0	0-0	0	0-0	0	0	6
Nordgren, Matt	1	0-0	0-0	0-0	0	0-0	0	0	6
Ogbonnaya, Chris	1	0-0	0-0	0-0	0	0-0	0	0	6
Ullman, Peter	1	0-0	0-0	0-0	0	0-0	0	0	6
Jones, Nate	1	0-0	0-0	0-0	0	0-0	0	0	6
Tweedie, Neale	1	0-0	0-0	0-0	0	0-0	0	0	6
Huff, Michael	1	0-0	0-0	0-0	0	0-0	0	0	6
Wright, Rodrique	1	0-0	0-0	0-0	0	0-0	0	0	6
McGee, Richmond	0	0-0	4-7	0-0	0	0-0	0	0	4
Team	0	0-0	0-0	0-0	0	0-0	0	1	2
Phillips, Kyle	0	0-0	1-1	0-0	0	0-0	0	0	1
Robison, Brian	0	0-0	0-0	0-0	0	0-0	0	0	0
Total	88	14-18	76-85	1-1	1	1-2	0	1	652
Opponents	25	14-20	21-22	0-1	0	0-2	0	0	213

Total Offense

Player	G	Plays	Rush	Pass	Total	Avg/G
Young, Vince	13	480	1,050	3,036	4,086	314.3
Charles, Jamaal	13	119	878	0	878	67.5
Taylor, Ramonce	13	76	513	0	513	39.5
Young, Selvin	11	96	461	0	461	41.9
Melton, Henry	13	87	432	0	432	33.2
Nordgren, Matt	12	23	38	47	85	7.1
Ogbonnaya, Chris	8	22	76	0	76	9.5
McCoy, Matt	4	6	31	0	31	7.8
Pittman, Billy	13	2	28	0	28	2.2
Houston, Michael	2	3	27	0	27	13.5
Hobbs, Antwaun	2	9	27	0	27	13.5
Ballew, Scott	2	4	14	0	14	7.0
Hall, Ahmard	13	1	10	0	10	0.8
Bobino, Rashad	13	1	6	0	6	0.5
Myers, Marcus	7	4	5	0	5	0.7
Team	13	8	-22	0	-22	-1.7
Total	13	941	3,574	3,083	6,657	512.1
Opponents	13	897	1,702	2,236	3,938	302.9

Field Goals

Player	FGM-FGA	Pct	01-19	20-29	30-39	40-49	50-99	Long	Blkd
Pino, David	14-18	77.8	0-0	4-4	4-7	6-6	0-1	46	1

Punting

Player	No.	Yds	Avg	Long	TB	FC	I20	Blkd
McGee, Richmond	35	1325	37.9	56	2	12	11	0
Johnson, Greg	2	84	42.0	48	0	0	1	0
Pino, David	1	35	35.0	35	0	0	1	0
Total	38	1,444	38.0	56	2	12	13	0
Opponents	89	3,485	39.2	58	5	16	17	6

All Purpose

Player	G	Rush	Rec	PR	KOR	IR	Total	Avg/G
Taylor, Ramonce	13	513	265	0	441	0	1,219	93.8
Young, Vince	13	1,050	0	0	0	0	1,050	80.8
Charles, Jamaal	13	878	157	0	0	0	1,035	79.6
Pittman, Billy	13	28	750	0	0	0	778	59.8
Thomas, David	13	0	613	0	0	0	613	47.2
Sweed, Limas	13	0	545	0	0	0	545	41.9
Ross, Aaron	13	0	0	500	0	40	540	41.5
Young, Selvin	11	461	21	0	0	0	482	43.8
Melton, Henry	13	432	0	0	0	0	432	33.2
Cosby, Quan	13	0	270	92	30	0	392	30.2
Carter, Brian	10	0	263	0	0	0	263	26.3
Brown, Tarell	13	0	0	0	108	11	119	9.2
Ogbonnaya, Chris	8	76	3	0	0	0	79	9.9
Griffin, Michael	13	0	0	68	0	0	68	5.2
Jones, Nate	13	0	67	0	0	0	67	5.2
Hall, Ahmard	13	10	42	0	14	0	66	5.1
Tweedie, Neale	13	0	49	0	0	0	49	3.8
Nordgren, Matt	12	38	0	0	0	0	38	3.2
McCoy, Matt	4	31	0	0	0	0	31	7.8
Harris, Aaron	13	0	0	0	0	30	30	2.3
Hobbs, Antwaun	2	27	0	0	0	0	27	13.5
Houston, Michael	2	27	0	0	0	0	27	13.5
Walker, George	5	0	22	0	0	0	22	4.4
Ballew, Scott	2	14	0	0	0	0	14	7.0
Gatewood, Tyrell	13	0	13	0	0	0	13	1.0
Huff, Michael	13	0	0	0	0	11	11	0.8
Griffin, Cedric	13	0	0	11	0	0	11	0.8
Bobino, Rashad	13	6	0	0	0	0	6	0.5
Myers, Marcus	7	5	0	0	0	0	5	0.7
Ullman, Peter	11	0	3	0	0	0	3	0.3
Kelson, Drew	13	0	0	0	0	-2	-2	-0.2
Team	13	-22	0	0	0	0	-22	-1.7
Total	13	3,574	3,083	671	593	90	8,011	616.2
Opponents	13	1,702	2,236	70	1,522	151	5,681	437.0

Individual Defensive Statistics

Player	GP	Solo	Ast	Total	TFL-Yds	No-Yds	Int-Yds	BrUp	Rcv-Yds	FF	Blkd Kick	Saf
Griffin, Michael	13	67	57	124	4-9	-	3-0	8	3-0	1	4	-
Huff, Michael	13	53	56	109	10-37	2.0-18	1-11	14	2-21	4	1	-
Harris, Aaron	13	57	34	91	12-50	4.0-22	1-30	3	-	2	-	-
Griffin, Cedric	13	48	38	86	1-2	-	-	15	1-0	2	-	-
Brown, Tarell	13	39	30	69	2-3	-	1-11	8	1-0	1	-	-
Killebrew, Robert	13	41	26	67	10-67	4.0-49	-	3	1-0	2	3	-
Ross, Aaron	13	35	27	62	3-40	-	3-40	9	-	-	-	-
Robison, Brian	12	35	23	58	15-80	7.0-62	-	4	2-9	3	1	-
Bobino, Rashad	13	33	20	53	7-21	2.0-14	-	1	1-0	1	-	-
Crowder, Tim	13	31	19	50	9-28	3.0-20	1-0	2	-	1	-	-
Okam, Frank	13	23	25	48	5-14	1.0-7	-	2	2-0	-	-	-
Wright, Rodrique	13	20	26	46	13-51	4.5-37	-	3	1-67	1	-	-
Kelson, Drew	13	17	19	36	2-7	1.0-6	1-(-2)	4	1-0	2	-	-
Dibbles, Larry	13	14	27	35	5-7	-	-	3	-	2	-	-
Griffin, Marcus	13	11	21	32	-	-	-	-	-	-	-	-
Orakpo, Brian	13	17	10	27	4-10	0.5-7	-	-	1-0	-	-	-
Lokey, Derek	11	9	8	17	2-16	1.0-15	-	-	-	-	-	-
Melton, Matt	13	6	10	16	-	-	-	-	-	-	-	-
Foreman, Eric	12	10	6	16	1-11	1.0-11	-	-	-	-	-	-
Foster, Brandon	13	9	7	16	1-1	-	-	-	-	1	-	-
Jackson, Erick	13	8	4	12	-	-	-	-	-	-	-	-
Meijer, Karim	11	3	9	12	-	-	-	-	-	-	-	-
Miller, Roy	10	3	7	10	-	-	-	1	-	-	-	-
Palmer, Ryan	11	5	3	8	-	-	-	-	-	-	-	-
Brown, Christopher	6	3	5	8	2-8	1.0-7	-	-	-	-	-	-
Lewis, Aaron	8	2	6	8	1-2	-	-	1	-	-	-	-
Johnson, Greg	12	5	2	7	-	-	-	-	-	-	-	-
Hall, Eric	11	6	1	7	4-13	1.0-8	-	-	-	-	-	-
Johnson, Braden	9	4	3	7	-	-	-	1	-	-	-	-
Marshall, Thomas	8	3	3	6	1-1	-	-	1	-	-	-	-
Janszen, Tully	13	1	4	5	1-1	-	-	-	-	-	-	-
Tatum, Bobby	9	-	4	4	-	-	-	1	-	-	-	-
Tiemann, Luke	4	-	3	3	-	-	-	-	-	-	-	-
Sweed, Limas	13	2	-	2	-	-	-	-	-	-	-	-
Thomas, David	13	-	2	2	-	-	-	-	-	-	-	-
Redwine, Nic	4	-	1	1	-	-	-	-	-	-	-	-
Young, Vince	13	1	-	1	-	-	-	-	-	-	-	-
Charles, Jamaal	13	1	-	1	-	-	-	-	-	-	-	-
McGee, Richmond	13	-	1	1	-	-	-	-	-	-	-	-
Taylor, Ramonce	13	1	-	1	-	-	-	-	-	-	-	-
Schroeder, Nick	13	-	1	1	-	-	-	-	-	-	-	-
Allen, Will	13	1	1	2	-	-	-	-	-	-	-	-
Ray, James	2	1	1	2	-	-	-	-	-	-	-	-
Campbell, Jeremy	4	1	1	2	-	-	-	-	-	-	-	-
Tweedie, Neale	13	1	1	2	-	-	-	-	-	-	-	-
Young, Selvin	11	1	1	2	-	-	-	-	-	-	-	-
Team	13	2	-	2	2-8	2.0-8	-	-	-	-	-	1
Total	13	630	542	1,172	116-451	34-268	11-90	85	16-97	23	9	1
Opponents	13	554	413	967	86-227	14-102	11-151	33	9-0	20	4	-

CREDITS

Austin American-Statesman

Assistant Sports Editors:
Rich Tijerina, James Wangemann and Art Moore

Page Designers and Copy Editors:
Tom Widlowski, Kevin Lyttle, Dave Doolittle,
Danny Douglas, Heath Shelby, John Agee,
Chris Hanna, Jason Whaley, Kevin Hargis
and Raeanne Martinez

Reporters:
Suzanne Halliburton, Cedric Golden,
Kevin Robbins, Mark Rosner, Randy Riggs,
Rick Cantu and John Maher

Columnist:
Kirk Bohls

Photo editors:
Jay Godwin and Rebecca McEntee

Photographers:
Deborah Cannon, Jay Janner, Ralph Barrera,
Brian Diggs, Matt Rourke, Larry Kolvoord,
Kelly West and Rodolfo Gonzalez

Photo staff:
Elena Grothe

OPPOSITE PAGE: Coach Mack Brown celebrates the Longhorns' Rose Bowl
victory with Vince Young, holding the championship trophy.
Ralph Barrera/American-Statesman

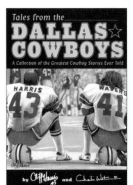
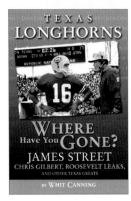
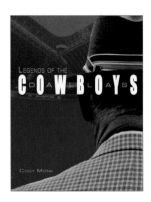